# VASCULAR SURGERY

Cavendish
Publishing
Limited

London • Sydney

**TITLES IN THE SERIES**

ACCIDENT AND EMERGENCY

CARDIOLOGY

CLINICAL CARE

DENTISTRY

EAR, NOSE AND THROAT

GENERAL PRACTICE

GENITO-URINARY

GYNAECOLOGY

MEDIATION AND ARBITRATION

NEPHROLOGY

NEUROLOGY

ONCOLOGY

OPHTHALMOLOGY

PSYCHIATRY

RESPIRATORY DISORDERS

UROLOGY

VASCULAR SURGERY

# VASCULAR SURGERY

John H Scurr
Consultant Surgeon

SERIES EDITOR
Dr Walter Scott, LLB (Hons),
MBBS, MRCGP, DObstRCOG

Cavendish
Publishing
Limited

London • Sydney

First published in Great Britain 1999 by Cavendish Publishing Limited, The Glass House, Wharton Street, London WC1X 9PX, United Kingdom.
Telephone: +44 (0) 171 278 8000     Facsimile: +44 (0) 171 278 8080
e-mail: info@cavendishpublishing.com
Visit our Home Page on http://www.cavendishpublishing.com


© Scurr, JH, 1999


All rights reserved. No part of this publication may be reproduced, stored in a retrieval system, or transmitted, in any form or by any means, electronic, mechanical, photocopying, recording, scanning or otherwise, except under the terms of the Copyright Designs and Patents Act 1988 or under the terms of a licence issued by the Copyright Licensing Agency, 90 Tottenham Court Road, London W1P 9HE, UK, without the permission in writing of the publisher.


Scurr, John
Vascular Surgery – (Medico-legal practitioner series)
1. Blood vessels – Surgery 2. Blood vessels – Surgery – Law
I. Title
617.4'13'002434

Every effort has been made to race all the copyright holders but, if any have been overlooked, the publishers will be pleased to make the necessary arrangement at the first opportunity.

ISBN 1 85941 158 4


Printed and bound in Great Britain

*I dedicate this book to the continuance of medical education and to my colleagues, whose unfortunate experiences and, often, real suffering provide the cases on which the experience to write this book was based; also, to those many friends in the legal profession who have encouraged and advised; and, finally, to those who support a common sense approach to the practice of medicine and just compensation to the true victims of medical accidents.*

# FOREWORD

When I first conceived the idea of the *Medico-Legal Practitioner Series* in the Summer of 1994, I had been preparing reports for lawyers on cases of alleged medical negligence for about five years. I had also been looking at other doctors' reports for the same length of time and it was becoming increasingly apparent to me that one of the lawyers' most difficult tasks was to understand the medical principles clearly. To be fair to the lawyers, there were some doctors who did not always make matters very clear. This, coupled with the difficulty which many doctors have in understanding the legal concept of negligence and related topics, merely served to compound the problem.

A little more than two years have now passed since I wrote the foreword for the initial launch of the series and, already, the number of titles available in the series has reached double figures with many more imminent. Therefore, this seems to be an appropriate moment to take stock of our efforts so far and to assess the way in which matters are likely to unfold in the future.

Since the publication of the first books in the series, there have been some exciting developments in the medico-legal scene and there can be no doubt that this is becoming an increasingly specialised field. That trend is likely to continue with the establishment of legal aid franchise firms of lawyers. Such firms will find it more and more necessary to identify strong cases and eliminate weak ones in an economical fashion and with as little risk as possible.

One important feature of the more recent titles in the series is the inclusion of case studies which are placed adjacent to the relevant parts of the text and are listed in a table for ease of reference. Most chapters have several examples of cases which have either settled in the plaintiff's favour or have fallen away because, perhaps, they were considered to be weak on negligence or causation. These studies give the reader a 'feel' for the work of the clinician and the difficulties which face him. The patient's expectations do not always correlate particularly well with the doctor's treatment plan, for example, in relation to consent, and such issues as this are often highlighted by the case studies.

The other interesting development in some of the newer titles is the coverage of areas that do not relate to clinical negligence. With the series becoming more comprehensive, we have felt able to expand into other medico-legal areas. Examples include *Respiratory Disorders* which deals with industrial lung disease and *Psychiatry* which covers testamentary capacity and the defence of insanity to criminal charges.

So much, then, for the latest developments in the *Medico-Legal Practitioner Series*. Our aim remains as it was at the outset with regard to uniformity of approach and clarity of presentation. In this way, I hope that our readers, mostly the practitioners who are engaged in unravelling the complexities of the medical evidence that is the subject of so much litigation, will continue to rely on us as an invaluable source of reference.

Walter Scott
Series Editor
Slough

# PREFACE

There can be few greater challenges left to a consultant surgeon than teaching. Teaching medical students, surgical trainees and colleagues provides a daily challenge from which we all learn. The opportunity to teach lawyers in a different discipline has provided a different opportunity to re-assess not only our teaching techniques but, also, our decisions about what information is really necessary. The ability to confuse by complex intellectual arguments must give way to a more systematic and logical approach. I have been greatly influenced by my own teachers and their ability to present difficult and complex issues in a simplified way, and to them I pay tribute. In this book, I have attempted to cover a large specialist area, covering many difficult concepts, concepts which my own colleagues sometimes have difficulty understanding. This publication is intended for lawyers with little or no medical experience but, at the same time, I hope that those with considerable medical knowledge will find the cases and some of the illustrations useful.

John H Scurr
London

# ACKNOWLEDGMENTS

With thanks to Dr Walter Scott for his ideas, encouragement and enthusiasm, to the editorial staff at Cavendish Publishing, to my own secretaries Vanessa and Emma for typing the manuscript, to Persephone Brigstocke for organising my time and, finally, to my colleagues and surgical trainees.

# CONTENTS

| | |
|---|---|
| *Foreword* | *vii* |
| *Preface* | *vix* |
| *Acknowledgments* | *xi* |
| *List of cases* | *xix* |

**1 ANATOMY**     1
- INTRODUCTION     1
- THE ARTERIAL SYSTEM     1
- THE VENOUS SYSTEM     2

**2 PHYSIOLOGY**     5
- INTRODUCTION     5
- THE HEART     5
- BLOOD VESSELS     6

**3 PATHOLOGY**     9
- INTRODUCTION     9
- TRAUMATIC DISORDERS     9
- INFECTIVE DISORDERS     9
- DEGENERATIVE DISORDERS     9
  - *Case – false aneurysm following trauma*     10
  - *Case – false aneurysm, secondary to infection following vascular surgery*     11
- NEOPLASTIC DISORDERS     12
- CONGENITAL DISORDERS     12

**4 PRESENTATION OF VASCULAR DISEASE**     13
- ARTERIAL DISEASE     13
- Embolisation     13
- *Case – acute arterial embolus*     14
- *Case – acute arterial embolus associated with severe illness*     15
- Diabetes     15
- Raynaud's disease     16
- *Case – vibration white finger*     16
- *Case – Raynaud's disease with amputation*     17
- *Case – Raynaud's disease, with complications following treatment*     17

|   |   |   |
|---|---|---|
|   | Buerger's disease | 18 |
|   | Trauma to arteries | 18 |
|   | *Case – vascular injury to the femoral artery* | 18 |
|   | *Case – vascular injury to the popliteal artery* | 19 |
|   | *Case – laparascopic injury to the right common iliac artery during general surgical procedure (I)* | 20 |
|   | *Case – laparoscopic injury to the right common iliac artery during general surgical procedure (II)* | 20 |
|   | *Case – injury to the right external iliac artery during gynaecological laparoscopic procedure* | 21 |
|   | VENOUS DISEASE | 22 |
|   | Varicose veins | 22 |
|   | Venous thrombosis | 22 |
|   | Trauma to veins | 23 |
| 5 | **INVESTIGATION OF ARTERIAL DISEASE** | 25 |
|   | INTRODUCTION | 25 |
|   | HISTORY | 26 |
|   | EXAMINATION | 26 |
|   | Inspection | 26 |
|   | Palpation | 27 |
|   | Auscultation | 27 |
|   | ROUTINE TESTS | 28 |
|   | DOPPLER/ULTRASOUND STETHOSCOPE | 28 |
|   | ANKLE BRACHIAL PRESSURE INDEX | 28 |
|   | DUPLEX ULTRASOUND IMAGING | 29 |
|   | ARTERIOGRAPHY | 31 |
|   | *Case – arteriography and complications with elective embolisation* | 32 |
|   | DIGITAL SUBTRACTION ANGIOGRAPHY | 35 |
|   | MAGNETIC RESONANCE IMAGING | 38 |
| 6 | **TREATMENT OF ARTERIAL DISEASE I** | 41 |
|   | INTRODUCTION | 41 |
|   | Management of a patient with intermittent claudication (arterial insufficiency in the legs) | 41 |
|   | ANGIOPLASTY | 42 |
|   | *Case – brachial artery injury following cardiac catheterisation (I)* | 46 |
|   | *Case – brachial artery injury following cardiac catheterisation (II)* | 47 |

| | | |
|---|---|---|
| | ENDARTERECTOMY | 49 |
| | Carotid arterial disease | 49 |
| | AORTIC ANEURYSM | 51 |
| | BYPASS SURGERY | 55 |
| | Arterio-iliac disease | 55 |
| | *Femoro-femoral bypass graft* | 55 |
| | *Aorto bifemoral bypass graft* | 56 |
| | Femoro-popliteal grafts | 57 |
| | AMPUTATION | 57 |
| | THE DIABETIC FOOT | 59 |
| | *Case – diabetes, with arterial insufficiency* | 61 |
| | *Case – diabetes, with local injury and arterial insufficiency* | 62 |
| **7** | **TREATMENT OF ARTERIAL DISEASE II** | **65** |
| | ACUTELY ISCHAEMIC LIMB | 65 |
| | Embolectomy | 65 |
| | Acute thrombosis | 66 |
| | SYMPATHECTOMY | 66 |
| | Cervical sympathectomy | 67 |
| | *Case – Nerve injury following cervical sympathectomy* | 68 |
| | *Case – Axillary hyperhidrosis (sympathetic overactivity)* | 69 |
| | Lumbar sympathectomy | 70 |
| | ARTERIO-VENOUS MALFORMATIONS | 70 |
| | VOLKMANN'S ISCHAEMIC CONTRACTURE | 71 |
| | *Case –Volkmann's ischaemic contracture* | 71 |
| | *Case – development of a compartment syndrome while using a tourniquet* | 72 |
| | *Case – compartment syndrome, secondary to compression* | 73 |
| | SURGICAL COMPLICATIONS | 73 |
| | FURTHER DEVELOPMENTS | 74 |
| **8** | **INVESTIGATION OF VENOUS DISEASE** | **77** |
| | INTRODUCTION | 77 |
| | HISTORY | 77 |
| | EXAMINATION | 77 |
| | Inspection | 78 |
| | Palpation | 78 |
| | Auscultation | 78 |

| | | |
|---|---|---|
| | DOPPLER/ULTRASOUND STETHOSCOPE | 78 |
| | PHOTOPLETHYSMOGRAPHY | 79 |
| | STRAIN GAUGE PLETHYSMOGRAPHY | 80 |
| | DUPLEX ULTRASOUND IMAGING | 82 |
| | VENOGRAPHY | 84 |
| 9 | **TREATMENT OF VENOUS DISEASE** | 87 |
| | DEEP VEIN THROMBOSIS | 87 |
| | Diagnosis of deep vein thrombosis | 88 |
| | Treatment of deep vein thrombosis | 89 |
| | Extensive deep vein thrombosis | 90 |
| | Prevention of deep vein thrombosis | 90 |
| | PULMONARY EMBOLISM | 92 |
| | Case – deep vein thrombosis, pulmonary embolism and bleeding complications | 93 |
| | Case – injury to leg, followed by deep vein thrombosis | 94 |
| | Case – leg injury, with superficial thrombophlebitis leading to deep vein thrombosis and fatal pulmonary embolism | 95 |
| | Case – road traffic accident with multiple injuries, deep vein thrombosis and pulmonary embolism | 96 |
| | Treatment of pulmonary embolism | 97 |
| | POST-THROMBOTIC LIMB | 98 |
| 10 | **VARICOSE VEINS** | 99 |
| | INTRODUCTION | 99 |
| | ASSESSMENT OF PATIENTS WITH VARICOSE VEINS | 100 |
| | SURGICAL TREATMENT OF VARICOSE VEINS | 100 |
| | Case – varicose veins, with sclerotherapy leading to superficial thrombophlebitis, deep vein thrombosis and fatal pulmonary embolism | 102 |
| | Case – treatment for varicose veins, leading to sensory nerve damage | 103 |
| | SCLEROTHERAPY | 103 |
| | MICROSCLEROTHERAPY | 105 |
| | Case – varicose veins and development of skin ulceration | 106 |
| | ALTERNATIVE FORMS OF TREATMENT | 107 |

| 11 | **VENOUS AND ARTERIAL RECONSTRUCTION** | 109 |
|---|---|---|
| | VENOUS TRAUMA | 109 |
| | *Case – treatment for varicose veins, leading to injury to deep veins* | 110 |
| | *Case – treatment for varicose veins, leading to injury to deep veins (bilateral)* | 111 |
| | Valve repair/replacement | 111 |
| | Venous bypass surgery | 112 |
| | ARTERIAL TRAUMA | 113 |
| | Management of a patient with an arterial injury | 114 |

*Appendix I – Medico-legal assessment of the vascular patient*     115

*Appendix II – Glossary of terms*     119

*Index*     125

# LIST OF CASES

| | | |
|---|---|---|
| 1 | False aneurysm following trauma | 10 |
| 2 | False aneurysm, secondary to infection following vascular surgery | 11 |
| 3 | Acute arterial embolus | 14 |
| 4 | Acute arterial embolus associated with severe illness | 15 |
| 5 | Vibration white finger | 16 |
| 6 | Raynaud's disease with amputation | 17 |
| 7 | Raynaud's disease, with complications following treatment | 17 |
| 8 | Vascular injury to the femoral artery | 18 |
| 9 | Vascular injury to the popliteal artery | 19 |
| 10 | Laparoscopic injury to the right common iliac artery during general surgical procedure (I) | 20 |
| 11 | Laparoscopic injury to the right common iliac artery during general surgical procedure (II) | 20 |
| 12 | Injury to the right external iliac artery during gynaecological laparoscopic procedure | 21 |
| 13 | Arteriography and complications with elective embolisation | 32 |
| 14 | Brachial artery injury following cardiac catheterisation (I) | 46 |
| 15 | Brachial artery injury following cardiac catheterisation (II) | 47 |
| 16 | Diabetes, with arterial insufficiency | 61 |
| 17 | Diabetes, with local injury and arterial insufficiency | 62 |
| 18 | Nerve injury following cervical sympathectomy | 68 |
| 19 | Axillary hyperhidrosis (sympathetic overactivity) | 69 |
| 20 | Volkmann's ischaemic contracture | 71 |
| 21 | Development of a compartment syndrome while using a tourniquet | 72 |
| 22 | Compartment syndrome, secondary to compression | 73 |
| 23 | Deep vein thrombosis, pulmonary embolism and bleeding complications | 93 |
| 24 | Injury to leg, followed by deep vein thrombosis | 94 |
| 25 | Leg injury, with superficial thrombophlebitis leading to deep vein thrombosis and fatal pulmonary embolism | 95 |
| 26 | Road traffic accident with multiple injuries, deep vein thrombosis and pulmonary embolism | 96 |
| 27 | Varicose veins, with sclerotherapy leading to superficial thrombophlebitis, deep vein thrombosis and fatal pulmonary embolism | 102 |
| 28 | Treatment for varicose veins, leading to sensory nerve damage | 103 |
| 29 | Varicose veins and development of skin ulceration | 106 |
| 30 | Treatment for varicose veins, leading to injury to deep veins | 110 |
| 31 | Treatment for varicose veins, leading to injury to deep veins (bilateral) | 111 |

# CHAPTER 1

# ANATOMY

## INTRODUCTION

William Harvey described the circulation of the blood in 1654. Before this, blood vessels had been described and careful anatomical diagrams constructed. Blood was thought to ebb and flow, providing basic nutrition to the body. Harvey recognised the importance of the heart as a pump, the arteries taking blood to the tissues and the veins returning blood from the tissues to the heart. Malpighi described capillaries which connect arteries and veins. They are responsible for the exchange of oxygen and nutrition. Two separate circulations exist, the circulation through the lungs, the pulmonary circulation, and the circulation through the body, the peripheral circulation. The heart consists of four chambers, two on the right and two on the left. The smaller chamber, the atrium, primes the major chamber, the ventricle, which then contracts to eject blood. Blood from the right side of the heart passes through the lungs where it receives oxygen, at the same time removing carbon dioxide. The blood returns from the lungs to the left side of the heart where it is pumped around the body. Arteries from the left side of the heart supply the brain, the chest, the abdomen and the limbs. Blood is collected via small veins which drain into larger veins, returning blood to the right side of the heart.

Arteries are thick walled and elastic. As the blood flows along an artery, the artery expands and contracts, pushing blood in a pulsatile fashion towards the tissues to be supplied. Blood in the arterial circulation is at relatively high pressure, blood in the venous circulation at low pressure. The veins have valves which allow the blood to flow in one direction only. Blood returns to the heart because of a negative sucking pressure created during respiration and due to muscular activity, which compresses the vein and squeezes the blood. The presence of valves ensures that the blood is squeezed in one direction, that is, towards the heart.

## THE ARTERIAL SYSTEM

The arterial system (see Figure 1.1) looks like a tree, with a trunk dividing into large branches and the large branches dividing into progressively smaller branches. The arterial anatomy is extremely constant, with very little variability, and the position of arteries is clearly defined. The limbs are each supplied by one major artery and most of the organs similarly have one major artery entering them. If this artery is blocked, the limb or organ will no longer receive a blood supply. This may result in the death of the organ or the limb unless an alternative route can be established.

## THE VENOUS SYSTEM

The veins are much more variable than arteries and duplication is not uncommon. The major vessels, the inferior and superior vena cava, are constant but veins in the periphery are extremely variable. Veins tend to run alongside arteries. Veins in the limbs are divided into superficial and deep veins, the deep veins providing the main route back to the heart. (see Figure 1.2) The limbs are enclosed by a non-elastic layer of fibrous tissue, like a sleeve. The deep veins are deep to this; the superficial veins, superficial. When muscles contract, the deep veins are compressed and blood is squeezed back towards the heart. The superficial veins drain into the deep veins and are protected by valves, ensuring a one way flow. Failure of these valves leads to high pressure in the superficial system, dilatation and elongation, a process leading to the development of varicose veins.

Anatomy

**Figure 1.1** The arterial tree

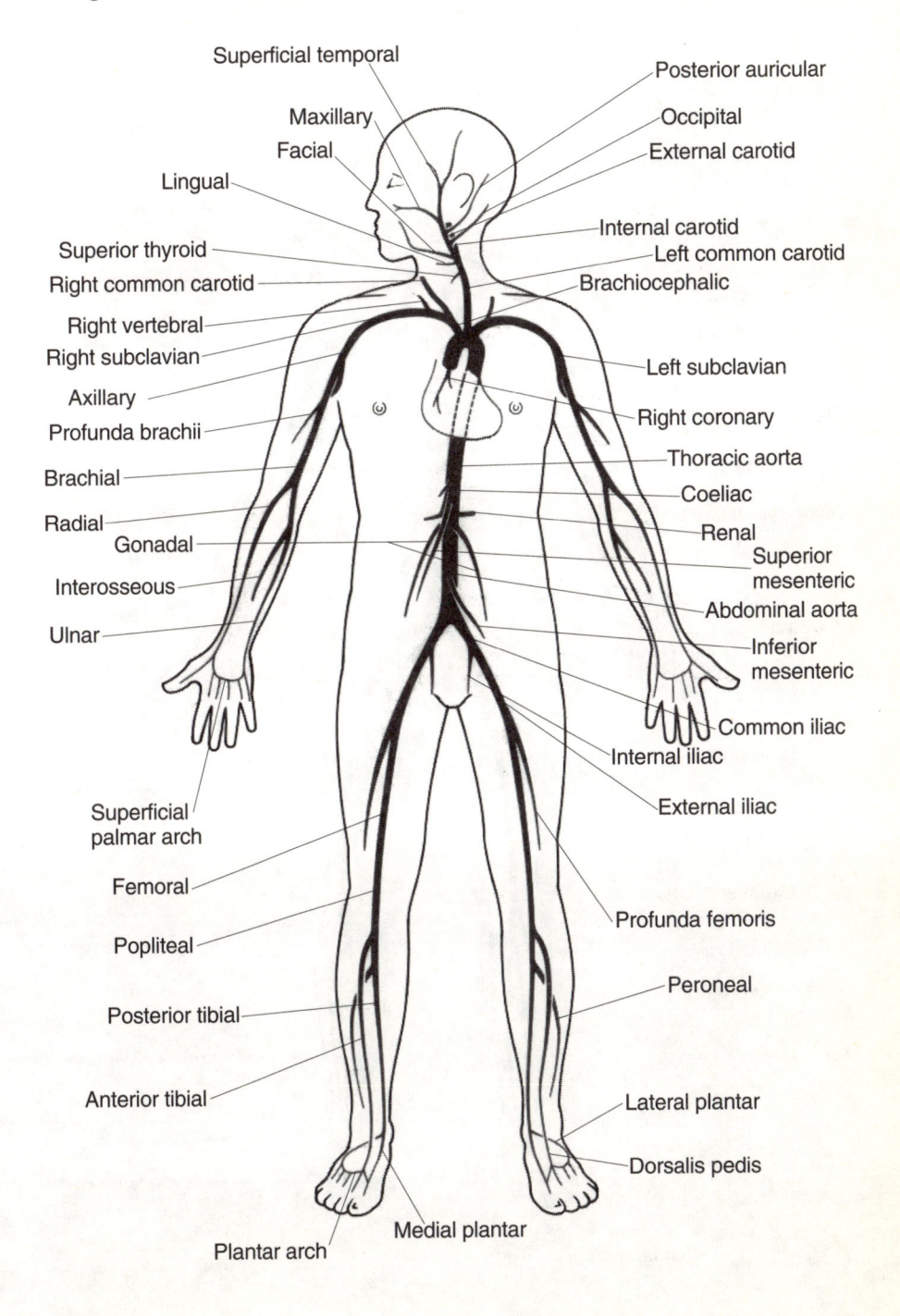

Vascular Surgery

**Figure 1.2** The venous tree

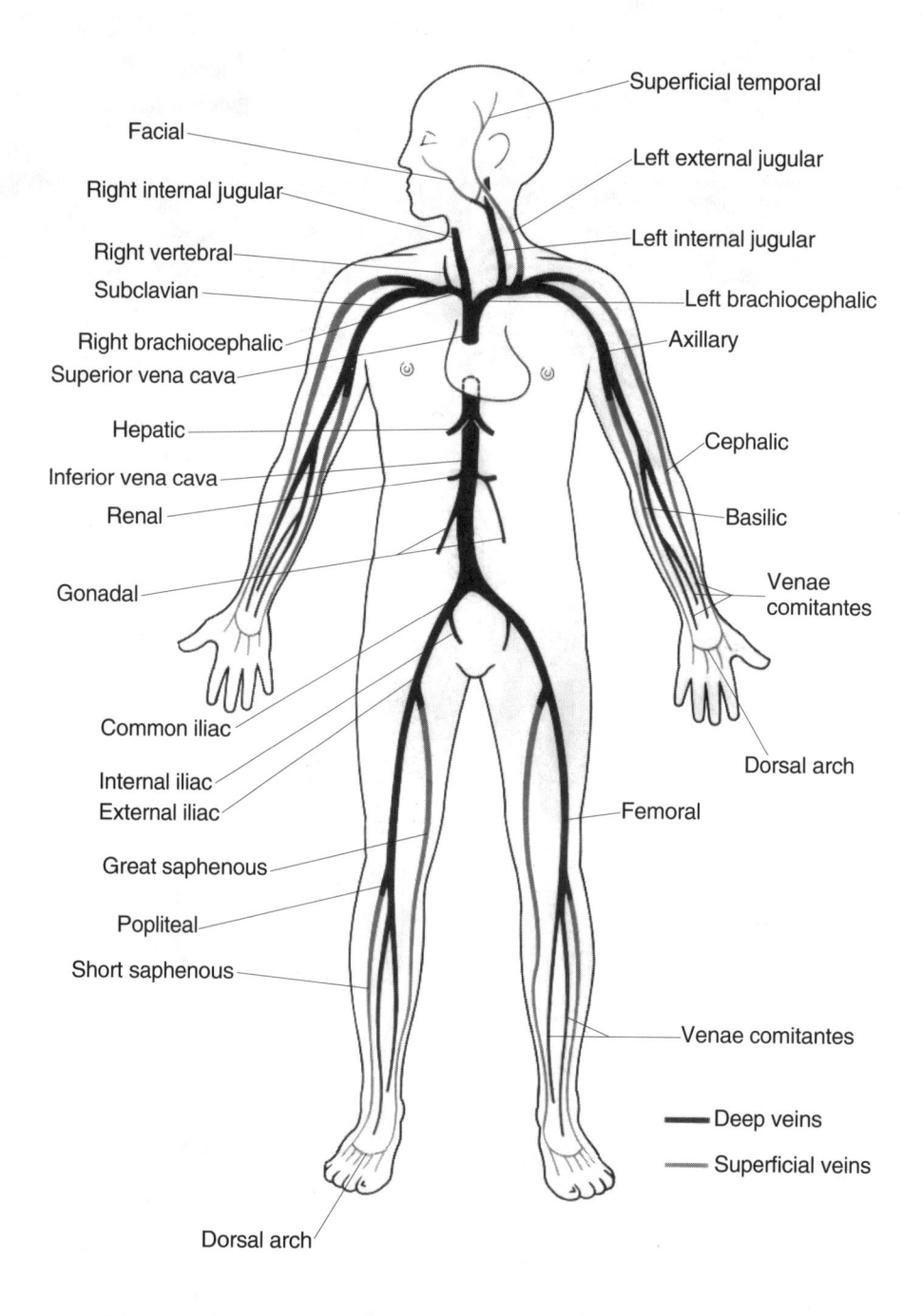

CHAPTER 2

# PHYSIOLOGY

## INTRODUCTION

The heart pumps blood, a fluid consisting of red cells, white cells and plasma, around the body. The red cells carry oxygen to the tissues and carbon dioxide from the tissues; the white cells are important in fighting disease and the plasma transports nutrients to the tissues and waste products from the tissues, which are metabolised in the liver or excreted by the kidneys. Blood remains fluid because of a fine balance between factors which cause the blood to clot and factors which cause clots to dissolve. When a small hole appears in the circulation, the body has the ability to repair this: first, by stopping the leak and, secondly, by repairing the hole. Leaks from the circulation are stopped by platelet plugs and the blood's ability to clot. When clotting does occur, the body has the ability to dissolve clots using an active fibrinolytic system. The body is better able to deal with clots from the venous side of the circulation than the arterial side.

## THE HEART

The key to the circulation is the heart. The heart appears as one organ but, in fact, is two separate pumps, a right and a left sided pump. It is a muscular structure which contracts rhythmically. The heart rate is determined by the body's requirement for oxygenation and nutrition. The normal heart rate is 80 beats per minute but heart rates as slow as 40 beats per minute or as fast as 200 beats per minute are commonly seen. The amount of blood put out by the heart depends on heart rate and the volume expressed per contraction. It is measured in litres per minute (l/min) and represents the cardiac output. The capacity of the ventricle is 200 ml. In a normal heart beat, the heart will eject 70 ml. If there is a greater requirement for more blood, then more complete emptying takes place, the heart ejecting from 150 to 170 ml. The normal cardiac output is 5 l/min, but this can increase to 30 l/min under exercise conditions. The increase is brought about by a more complete emptying of the pump and an increased rate of contraction. The arterial blood pressure is determined by the cardiac output and the peripheral resistance. If the peripheral resistance to flow increases, then the blood pressure will rise. If the cardiac output decreases with no change in peripheral resistance, blood pressure will fall. If a patient suddenly loses blood as a result of an accident, the cardiac output and the blood pressure fall. By increasing peripheral resistance, the blood pressure can be maintained, but only for a limited period of time.

At any one time, one-fifth of the circulation is in the arteries and four-fifths of the circulation is in the veins. The veins have great capacity and, if blood is lost from the circulation, by contracting the veins, pressure can be maintained within the circulation. It is possible to lose one litre of blood quite quickly without it having a serious effect on blood pressure. If two or more litres of blood are lost quite quickly, then there will be an initial fall in the blood pressure until the volume of the circulation can be made up by drawing fluid from other tissues into the circulation. Drawing fluid into the circulation dilutes the red blood cells, resulting in anaemia.

Blood pressure is maintained by baro receptors. These are pressure sensitive nerves located in the base of the neck and upper thorax. Other receptors measure oxygen and carbon dioxide levels to adjust the rate of blood flow and the rate of breathing.

As stated above, the heart is, in fact, two separate pumps. It is important that both pumps pump blood at the same rate to avoid blood either pooling in the lungs or pooling in the peripheral circulation, leading to a condition known as cardiac failure. When blood pools in the lungs, we refer to it as congestive cardiac failure, the patient presenting with acute shortness of breath. In normal healthy individuals, mechanisms exist whereby the balance is maintained.

## BLOOD VESSELS

The blood vessels can transport blood to and from the heart. The blood vessels taking blood from the heart are arteries. The blood vessels taking blood back to the heart are veins. The arteries are elastic, expanding when the blood flows from the heart and then contracting. It is this expansile nature of the artery which is responsible for the pulse which can be easily felt in normal vessels.

The veins have a very thin muscular wall. The veins contain valves, so the blood flows in one direction. The blood is pumped from the heart and returned via the venous pumps.

The are many venous pumps, which work when the muscles surrounding the veins contract. When the muscles surrounding a vein contract, the vein becomes compressed and blood flows in one direction.

Four-fifths of the blood's volume is within the veins. The veins act as capacitance vessels, so that, if a patient loses a considerable quantity of blood, by constricting, the veins can maintain the circulation.

Blood in the arteries contains high levels of oxygen, while blood in the veins contains relatively low levels of oxygen and increased levels of carbon dioxide. Carbon dioxide is removed from the blood in the lungs and oxygen is added. The arteries contain oxygenated blood and the veins, de-oxygenated blood. The only exceptions to this are the pulmonary artery, which takes de-oxygenated blood from the heart to the lungs, and the pulmonary vein, which takes oxygenated blood from the lungs back to the heart.

**Figure 2.1**   **Diagram of the heart and circulation**

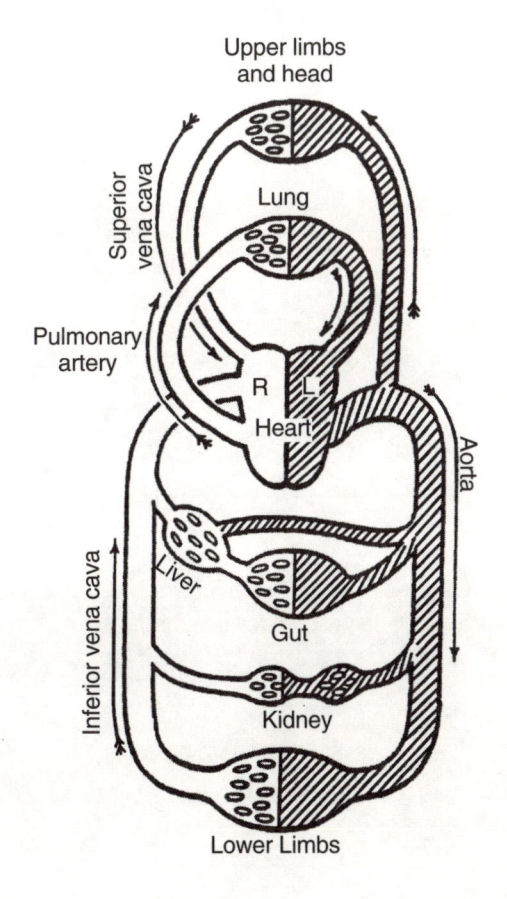

# CHAPTER 3

# PATHOLOGY

## INTRODUCTION

The heart, the arteries and the veins all form part of the circulation. Only pathology affecting the arteries and veins will be considered in this chapter. Arteries and veins are affected by a number of disease processes. These disease processes can be summarised as traumatic, infective, degenerative, neoplastic and congenital.

## TRAUMATIC DISORDERS

Blunt, sharp or surgical trauma is increasing. Sharp trauma, that is, stabbings and gunshot injuries, are usually easily recognised. Blunt trauma may cause damage to the arterial lining, allowing it to separate and block the artery. Either direct trauma, from a blow, or indirect trauma, secondary to an orthopaedic injury, may occur. Over-extension of joints may result in small branches detaching and the development of aneurysms. Both arteries and veins can be damaged accidentally during surgical procedures. Failure to recognise this damage can result in the development of symptoms, sometimes very rapidly but, at other times, delayed for weeks or months.

## INFECTIVE DISORDERS

Infection can get into the blood stream and result in septicaemia. More commonly, areas of localised disease, within either the heart or major arteries, become colonised with bacteria. Fragments may separate, before lodging in the peripheral circulation and either blocking the artery or resulting in the development of an infective aneurysm.

## DEGENERATIVE DISORDERS

With ageing, the arterial wall becomes harder, less elastic and weakened. This process is known as arteriosclerosis and may lead to narrowing of the arteries (stenotic disease) or dilatation of the arteries due to weakening (aneurysm formation). Narrowing of the arteries leads to a restriction of blood flow, which may, in the first instance, limit exercise and, later on, threaten the viability of the limb.

Aneurysms may be true or false. A true aneurysm is a weakness of the wall, which allows the artery to distend in the same way that a balloon enlarges when inflated. A true aneurysm has a thin arterial wall. A false aneurysm occurs when an artery has been punctured or a small branch has been avulsed. Blood spills from the artery and is contained by surrounding tissues, usually muscles or fascia.

As the blood flows through an aneurysm, clot is usually laid down in the cavity. This clot may detach, travelling towards the edge of the body (periphery) as an embolus and, thus, blocking the circulation.

The veins are relatively thin walled but are also subject to degenerative changes. With age, the dilated veins becoming more tortuous. The dilatation is probably due to weakened walls and gives rise to valvular incompetence, reducing the efficiency of the veins in returning the blood to the heart.

Spontaneous clotting can occur within the veins, leading to partial or complete obstruction. If clots cause obstruction to major veins, particularly in the lower legs, swelling may occur. If the clots are not firmly adherent to the vein walls, they can break off and travel to the lung as an embolus. Small emboli may be asymptomatic but larger emboli can cause serious irregularities in the heart or even completely block the flow of blood through the lungs, resulting in death. Emboli arising in the venous system travel to the right side of the heart and get trapped in the lungs. These clots cannot get into the arterial circulation and, therefore, do not cause stroke or arterial emboli. Rarely, abnormalities, such as a hole in the heart, can allow a clot to travel from the right side to the left side. Arterial emboli must arise either in the heart or the major arteries and can give rise to strokes, where the arterial circulation to the brain becomes occluded. Strokes are caused either by bleeding into the brain or by a blockage in the circulation, as a result either of an embolus or of spontaneous thrombosis in an artery that has been narrowed.

*Case*

*False aneurysm following trauma*

Mr W fell, injuring his right shoulder. Following the fall, he could not move the shoulder fully and was referred by his general practitioner to hospital to undergo an X-ray investigation. X-rays of the shoulder and clavicle revealed no fracture and there were no neurological abnormalities noted. There was no record of the circulation having been checked. Mr W returned home with pain-relieving tablets.

Ten days after the fall, he complained to his general practitioner of extensive bruising over the upper arm. The general practitioner examined him and noticed the presence of very extensive bruising and swelling beneath the clavicle. The general practitioner requested a further opinion from the hospital.

On examination, he was noted to have a pulsatile swelling just beneath the clavicle. Arteriography revealed the presence of a false aneurysm. Mr W then underwent surgery to repair this. Mr W alleged the hospital were neglectful for missing this injury when he first presented.

The initial injury was probably associated with a small branch of the subclavian artery, the main artery supplying the arm, being avulsed. This would have led to some bleeding at the time of the injury but not sufficient to cause any obvious signs.

Although no attempt to examine the circulation was carried out, even if it had been, there would have been no abnormal findings.

When a small branch has avulsed from the side of the artery, the hole usually goes into spasm and seals spontaneously.

In this case, the hole then started to bleed and a false aneurysm developed. A certain amount of leakage occurred, resulting in extensive bruising in the upper arm.

The diagnosis was made when Mr W complained to his general practitioner on the second occasion and appropriate treatment carried out.

This case did not proceed.

*Case*

*False aneurysm, secondary to infection following vascular surgery*

Mr S underwent successful bypass surgery for intermittent claudication in his right leg. The operation involved inserting an artificial graft between the groin and the knee.

Following the operation, the patient developed an infection in the groin. This was treated with antibiotics and, at first, appeared to resolve. Three weeks after the operation, the patient re-presented with a painful swelling in the groin. The swelling was pulsatile and a diagnosis of a false aneurysm was made. Further investigations revealed infection in the groin, affecting the graft. Re-exploration of the groin confirmed infection and a false aneurysm. The graft was removed and further graft inserted, avoiding the previous operation site.

The circulation was successfully restored to the limb and the patient made a good recovery. The patient was told by one of the nurses that the infection was caused by a Methicillin resistant staphylococcus aureus (MRSA) and that he was the fifth patient on the ward to have been infected.

The patient alleged that he should not have undergone the surgical procedure in the presence of known infections.

Infection is always a risk with vascular patients because the circulation to the limb is often compromised. The use of prosthetic materials means that, if an infection takes place, antibiotics may fail to work. When this case was investigated, it was found that there was no substance in the allegation; however, there were many other cases of MRSA infection and the conclusion was that this was an unfortunate, but well recognised, complication. The complication of a false aneurysm was recognised and managed appropriately.

The outcome was the same as it would have been without the second operation and the case was therefore discontinued.

## NEOPLASTIC DISORDERS

Abnormalities of the arterial wall do occur, leading to swelling (tumours). These tumours may arise from nerve tissue within the arterial wall and may result in arterial occlusion, for example, carotid body tumour.

## CONGENITAL DISORDERS

Congenital abnormalities may occur in both the arterial and the venous system. The commonest arterial abnormality is an arteriovenous malformation. This may present as a simple birthmark, or it can present as a very complicated vascular structure, which can affect limb growth or the development of organs.

# CHAPTER 4

# PRESENTATION OF VASCULAR DISEASE

## ARTERIAL DISEASE

Arterial disease results in a reduction of blood flow to either an organ or a limb. The commonest forms of presentation are cerebrovascular disease, cardiac disease or peripheral vascular disease (blood flow to the limbs). Narrowing of the arteries to other organs may also present with serious symptoms. If the blood supply to the one of the kidneys is seriously affected, then a patient may present with raised blood pressure. A patient with cerebrovascular disease may present with a stroke, causing paralysis or loss of function. Mini strokes or transient ischaemic attacks (TIAs) may provide warning symptoms. A transient ischaemic attack is any neurological disturbance which lasts less than 24 hours. Patients presenting in this way should be investigated, and if there is an underlying cause it may be amenable to treatment. Patients with arterial disease may also have problems affecting the heart. Whilst that does not form part of this book, it is important to remember that all systems can be affected and all systems may need investigating prior to carrying out treatment.

A patient with narrowing of the arteries of the leg will usually present with intermittent claudication. Claudication is pain in the leg, causing the patient to limp. Typically a patient is able to walk a fixed distance, anything from 50 to several hundred yards, before experiencing severe pain in the muscles in the leg. If the patient stands still for a few minutes, the pain goes and the patient can walk the same distance again. Claudication occurs during exercise because the flow of blood into the leg is insufficient to meet the energy requirements.

Rest pain is a more serious condition and occurs even when the patient is sitting still. Rest pain typically affects the great toe first, then the forefoot, before affecting the leg. The tissues furthest from the heart are most severely affected. Even at rest, there is insufficient blood supply to keep the tissues going and the patient is in serious danger of losing the leg.

### Embolisation

A patient who complains of sudden onset of pain and pallor (where the limb becomes very pale) should be considered a vascular emergency. The sudden onset of pain and pallor suggests that the circulation to the limb might be blocked. If nothing is done about it, there is a real risk of long term damage to the limb. An embolus is a piece of solid material, often a blood clot, which dislodges and travels through the circulation until it becomes jammed when the circulation narrows. Once the circulation is blocked, further clotting may occur until the circulation is completely occluded with sludge. When a patient presents with these signs and symptoms, urgent investigations and treatment are essential. The commonest form of embolism is a blood clot, but pieces of vessel wall affected by atheroma, hardening of the arteries or infected material can also embolise.

*Case*

## Acute arterial embolus

Mr M was admitted to hospital as an emergency with a one day history of a tingling sensation in the right leg associated with pallor. On examination, no pulses were felt in the right leg, and Mr M was commenced on subcutaneous heparin. The colour was thought to have improved by the following day and Mr M was allowed home with a provisional diagnosis of arterial spasm. However, he was re-admitted as an emergency two weeks later with 'spasm' in the right groin, associated with right leg swelling. On examination, he appeared to have some cellulitis of the leg; again, no peripheral pulses were palpable, and the right foot was cooler than the left. On this occasion, Mr M was given one dose of intravenous heparin and commenced on flucloxacillin and benzyl penicillin. He was allowed home the following day with a diagnosis of cellulitis but was re-admitted at the request of his general practitioner two weeks later with no improvement in his symptoms. He was again placed on subcutaneous heparin and treated with bed rest and elevation. At this stage, he was thought to have an arterial embolus and underwent an echocardiogram and abdominal ultrasound scan. He was discharged home one week later and re-admitted as a day case for a right lumbar sympathectomy. Mr M was seen in clinic shortly after, when it was noted there was no improvement in his symptoms and an X-ray of his right leg was performed, subsequently reported as showing osteomyelitis. In view of this, he was referred to an orthopaedic consultant surgeon and admitted under his care. By this stage, he had gangrene of his right forefoot, and underwent a through knee amputation.

When Mr M presented, he had signs and symptoms of vascular insufficiency. He should have undergone arteriography and, at that stage, should have either undergone an embolectomy or have been treated with thrombolytic therapy.

By failing to investigate and make the diagnosis, irreversible changes occurred in the leg, which were made worse by infection. Even when the diagnosis of arterial embolus was made, he did not undergo arteriography.

Presentation of Vascular Disease

An X-ray on his leg performed in out-patients showed evidence of osteomyelitis, but this was missed by the doctors in the clinic.

By the time the diagnosis became apparent, Mr M had gangrene in his right forefoot and had to undergo a through knee amputation.

With proper treatment, amputation would have been avoided.

This case has settled and liability has been admitted but the full details are unknown.

*Case*

*Acute arterial embolus associated with severe illness*

Mr TB consulted his general practitioner with a three day history of diarrhoea. He was seen on three further occasions, his diarrhoea not settling, and was admitted as an emergency under the care of the physicians. His condition failed to settle and a surgical review was sought. This led to an urgent laparotomy and total colectomy for toxic megacolon. Post-operatively he was managed on the intensive care unit and his initial recovery appeared to have been fairly uneventful. However, he developed a large negative fluid balance, culminating in the development of acute renal failure. The acute renal failure was treated by haemodialysis. The same day he was noted to have had a cold right foot since 2 am that day, thought possibly to be due to arterial embolism. Mr TB had been placed on subcutaneous heparin following his first operation, and this was changed for an intravenous heparin infusion. An attempted femoral and iliac embolectomy was carried out but this failed to restore normal flow and a below knee amputation was then performed.

Acute arterial embolus in a very sick patient is a well recognised complication. This man's post-operative fluid balance was not well controlled and, as a result, he became haemoconcentrated and developed renal failure.

Despite good treatment for his renal failure, it was not possible to restore the circulation to his leg. Although the diagnosis of an acute arterial occlusion was made and he received appropriate treatment, he still went on to undergo an amputation.

The defendants admitted liability and a settlement was achieved without going to court. Details are unknown.

## Diabetes

Diabetes is a condition where patients have difficulty in controlling their blood sugar levels. Blood sugar is controlled by insulin, a hormone produced in the pancreas. If the blood sugar is not maintained within a normal range, this affects other tissues within the body, including the blood vessels and nerves. Diabetic patients are known to have an increased incidence of arteriosclerotic disease. Arteriosclerotic disease is a condition where the artery becomes hardened and narrowed. This can affect all the vessels, resulting in a reduced circulation to a limb. Diabetic patients also have problems with the small vessels in the skin and muscles, called diabetic microangiopathy. Diabetic patients may present with combined vascular and neurological problems. The sensation in the feet is reduced, making the patients prone to injuries. These injuries can lead to ulceration with a loss of a toe, part of the foot or part of the limb. Diabetic patients with injuries and ulcers need to be investigated and then treated with great care.

Diabetic patients are more prone to infection, partly because of their raised blood sugar levels and partly because of their inability to fight infection due to the reduced circulation.

## Raynaud's disease

Raynaud's disease is a vaso-spastic condition, more common in women than men, but results from small vessels going into spasm. It commonly affects the fingers in the hands and can also affect the feet. The spasm may be brought on by vibration or cold and can result in serious skin changes and the loss of fingers. Sometimes this condition is associated with other medical problems. These medical problems include connective tissue disorders and rheumatoid arthritis. Although all these patients are investigated, in many, no specific underlying cause is found.

*Case*

*Vibration white finger*

Mr F consulted his general practitioner in January 1992 with problems in his left hand. At that stage, the diagnosis of Raynaud's phenomena was made. Two months after this he was commenced on nifedipine. At this stage, the possible link between his occupation, an operator of a road hammer drill, and the Raynaud's phenomena was considered. He underwent a series of investigations, which excluded any other cause for the Raynaud's phenomena. These investigations included exclusion of underlying collagen disorders. The conclusion was that his condition probably was related to the excessive use of a hammer drill.

This case was settled for £77,500 without going to court.

*Case*

## Raynaud's disease with amputation

Mrs J presented to her general practitioner with polyarthralgia and pain and swelling of the middle three toes of the right foot. There was no relevant past medical history. The general practitioner made a diagnosis of Raynaud's disease and referred her to hospital. The possibility of an underlying connective tissue disorder was raised and she underwent a series of investigations. During the course of these investigations, she went on to develop infection in the second and third toes. She received no specific treatment at this stage and her condition deteriorated rapidly. This culminated in her undergoing a right forefoot amputation.

There was no significant delay in her presentation and the general practitioner referring her to hospital. Investigations carried out at the hospital were comprehensive. They were carried out on an out-patients basis and Mrs J developed her infection whilst at home.

She did not seek medical help immediately and, as a result of this, the infection got out of control. Mrs J considered that with appropriate treatment she would not have required an amputation. When she did seek medical help she was immediately admitted and underwent appropriate treatment. She has made a good recovery and suffers very little in the way of disability.

Following receipt of medical reports, this case was discontinued.

*Case*

## Raynaud's disease, with complications following treatment

Mr W presented to his general practitioner with the features of Raynaud's syndrome in the right hand. He was investigated and no specific cause was found for this. He received a course of medical treatment, which was unsuccessful, and a decision was made to perform a right cervical sympathectomy.

Having undergone a right cervical sympathectomy, Mr W noted pain in his right hand and forearm, associated with some loss of function. Further investigations revealed an injury to the brachial plexus caused during the cervical sympathectomy procedure.

Raynaud's disease is generally treated medically. There are a few indications where a cervical sympathectomy may be carried out but the number of indications for this procedure have reduced.

Vascular Surgery

In this case, there probably were indications to carry out the cervical sympathectomy. During the course of the operation, damage to the brachial plexus, which runs in close proximity to the cervical sympathetic chain in the neck, occurred. This operation was carried out through the base of the neck.

Although there were clear indications to carry out the operation, the operation itself was not performed in a competent manner.

Liability was admitted and the case settled, but no details of the quantum were released.

## Buerger's disease

This is a serious condition which affects young men, nearly all of whom are smokers. It is a thrombo obliterative disease (clotting occurs in the small arteries), leading to gangrenous changes (death of the tissue) affecting the hands and feet, often resulting in amputation.

## Trauma to arteries

Damage to arteries can occur as a result of blunt or sharp trauma and may occur as a consequence of surgical procedures. Any patient sustaining a limb injury should have the circulation examined.

The arteries run very close to the long bones in the limbs, and when the bones are broken, the arteries can be damaged. The artery may appear intact, but the lining can crack, roll up and cause a blockage. If an artery is completely divided, it will contract and the amount of blood loss may be relatively small. Conversely, partial damage to the artery can result in a considerable amount of blood loss. Any patient who has suffered an injury to a limb should be examined fully and that includes examining for the presence of pulses. If pulses are absent, and the limb cold and pale, then the circulation should be investigated immediately. Any injury which involves dislocation of a joint, again may be associated with arterial damage. If the dislocation is corrected, the circulation may be restored. Observations should continue to make sure that the circulation does not then become occluded.

*Case*

*Vascular injury to the femoral artery*

A motorcyclist sustained a fracture to the lower third of his right femur and was admitted to hospital, where an X-ray revealed a fractured femur. This was treated with traction. The admitting houseman recorded a pale, cold foot, the dorsalis pedis pulse present and the posterior tibial pulse absent. There were no further investigations. Eighteen hours after admission, the patient complained of pain in the calf and foot and was seen by the orthopaedic registrar. He questioned the possibility of vascular injury and the patient was seen by a vascular surgeon. An arteriogram showed disruption to the superficial femoral artery just above fracture site. Exploration of the femoral artery was undertaken and intimal dissection was noted. Repair was undertaken, along with decompression of all three compartments in the lower leg. Pulses returned, but the patient went on to lose all the muscles and developed gangrenous changes in the skin, leading to an above knee amputation.

In this case, the orthopaedic surgeon failed to appreciate that there was evidence of a vascular injury, despite clear clinical signs on admission. A vascular opinion was not obtained on admission and there was a delayed vascular reconstruction, by which time, irreversible changes had occurred in the leg, leading to amputation. It is probable that the houseman could not actually feel the dorsalis pedis pulse. Simple examination with a Doppler probe would have proven that it was absent and led to an urgent vascular referral. This case was not defended.

*Case*

### Vascular injury to the popliteal artery

A young lady slipped and fell at work, injuring her left knee. She was taken by ambulance to the accident and emergency department at the local hospital, where she was admitted under the care of a consultant orthopaedic surgeon. On admission, it was noted that peripheral pulses were not present below the knee and the patient was reviewed by a consultant surgeon, who noted that there was apparently no problem with viability of the limb and no surgical exploration was justified. Accordingly, she was transferred to a ward where she was treated conservatively with elevation of the limb. It was noted that the patient was very pale, with a marked tachycardia, and she was noted to have a haemoglobin of only 5 g/dl (the normal amount being 12–18 g/dl), requiring six units of blood transfusion. She continued to be reviewed both by the orthopaedic and surgical teams and the conservative management was continued. However, she developed blistering over the back of the knee, followed by decreased sensation in movement of the lower limb, such that, after a month, it was decided that the leg was no longer salvageable and amputation should be performed. An above knee amputation was carried out, with subsequent closure of the stump. The patient was allowed home and has since been referred to a disablement services centre for fitting of an artificial limb.

The plaintiff's case was that she sustained an injury to the artery behind the knee. If this injury had been recognised and treated appropriately, she would not have required an amputation. There were two defendants. The first defendant, the shop where the accident occurred, was found liable for the accident but argued that, if she had received proper treatment, she would not have lost her leg. The second defendant, the hospital, argued that the arterial injury was part of a generalised medical problem affecting the leg and that she would have inevitably lost the leg. The judge found in favour of the plaintiff and accepted that, with proper management, the leg could have been saved.

*Case*

## Laparoscopic injury to the right common iliac artery during general surgical procedure (I)

A 38 year old man underwent laparoscopic cholecystectomy for symptomatic chronic cholecystitis. During the procedure, a trocar was accidentally inserted through the right common iliac artery. This resulted in catastrophic collapse of the patient, who required urgent resuscitation. The laceration required an aorto right femoral bypass. He made an uncomplicated post-operative recovery. Six weeks later, he underwent conventional cholecystectomy with no complications.

The patient sustained a serious injury. Given that the iliac artery is a fixed structure at the back of the abdomen, damage to this should not occur. The surgeon, in his defence, attempted to blame the trocar and cannula, which have now been tested and found not to be at fault.

Even if the port was at fault, there could be no defence for inserting it in such a way as to damage structures at the back of the abdomen.

Although the patient has made a full recovery, he is left with a major abdominal incision and a synthetic bypass graft. The risk of this graft occluding is small.

This case is currently being discussed and early indications suggest that a settlement will be achieved.

*Case*

## Laparoscopic injury to the right common iliac artery during general surgical procedure (II)

A 28 year old lady with a history of abdominal pain was referred privately by her general practitioner to a consultant gastroenterologist. The general practitioner thought the pain was probably due to biliary colic, and an ultrasound scan confirmed gall stones. He then referred her on the NHS to a consultant surgeon at the local hospital. She was reviewed, when it was noted that she was suitable for laparoscopic cholecystectomy. The patient was then admitted to another hospital, undergoing laparoscopic cholecystectomy the following day. During this procedure, the surgeon noted arterial bleeding within the peritoneal cavity and he carried out a laparotomy through a lower midline incision, repairing a puncture wound to the internal iliac artery. Routine open cholecystectomy was then performed. The patient made a fairly uneventful recovery from this operation, being discharged home. She was subsequently reviewed by a consultant surgeon one month later, when she was complaining of abdominal pain, distension and vomiting, and was admitted to the hospital the following day for observation. During this stay, she was found to be constipated, and a barium meal and follow through were performed, which were normal. She was allowed home one week later but subsequently referred back to the consultant gastroenterologist with persistence of her symptoms; a diagnosis of irritable bowel syndrome was made.

It is probable that the arterial damage occurred during the insertion of the Verres needle. This is the needle which is used to introduce the gas to create the pneumoperitoneum. Although damage to mesenteric vessels has been described, damage to major vessels at the back of the abdomen should not occur. These vessels are in a fixed position and care must be taken when introducing these needles to avoid aiming at them.

The damage was recognised immediately and repaired. Most of the patient's persistent symptoms were unrelated to the accident.

This case settled for £15,000.

*Case*

## Injury to the right external iliac artery during gynaecological laparoscopic procedure

A patient with pelvic and abdominal pain was admitted to hospital to undergo a laparoscopy, and dilatation and curettage. Whilst undergoing this procedure, the right external iliac artery was inadvertently damaged during the division of adhesions. An immediate laparotomy was carried out to control the bleeding. The patient required an intravenous blood transfusion and an arterial surgeon was called to assist in the repair of the artery using a venous patch.

Post-operatively, the patient made a reasonably straightforward physical recovery, albeit with an area numbness in the right upper thigh. However, she remained in an emotionally distressed state and there were difficulties with the nursing and medical staff. She was discharged home.

Damage to the right external iliac artery occurred during division of adhesions. A gynaecological opinion was obtained, suggesting that division of adhesions was an appropriate procedure.

It would have to be accepted when dividing adhesions that there is a risk of damage to neighbouring structures. This risk is small but, when it occurs, provided it is recognised and treated appropriately, this is consistent with standard medical practice.

The patient continued to complain of symptoms. The majority of the patient's complaint appeared to be related to difficulties in communication between the nursing and medical staff. There was a complete breakdown in communications and this undoubtedly led to the claim.

The case settled, but neither the solicitor nor the client were prepared to discuss the details.

# VENOUS DISEASE

## Varicose veins

Varicose veins are tortuous undilated superficial veins; they are extremely common, affecting 30% of the population. Seventy-five per cent of the patients presenting with varicose veins are women, the majority of patients presenting with a combination of symptoms (aching, swelling, pain, restlessness) and dissatisfaction with the appearance of their leg (cosmetic concerns). Although varicose veins are commonly perceived as being principally cosmetic, they get progressively worse and may end up leading to skin thickening and skin ulceration. The skin thickening is due to a collection of blood and the local tissues reacting to it. This reaction is caused by an accumulation of white blood cells, which in turn lead to skin ulceration. One hundred thousand people in the UK have skin ulcers. Half of these are due to varicose veins and, if the patients receive treatment, the ulcer will heal, never to return again.

## Venous thrombosis

Venous thrombosis may occur following an illness and hospitalisation, or can occur spontaneously. The classic signs and symptoms include swelling of the leg, pain, redness, dilatation of the superficial veins and a low grade temperature. More than 50% of patients developing a clot in the leg have no signs at all. In 20% of those patients with the classical signs and symptoms of a deep vein thrombosis, the cause of leg swelling is due to something else, the veins subsequently proving to be entirely normal. This clearly presents diagnostic problems which may then affect treatment.

## Trauma to veins

Damage to the veins seldom causes a serious problem. Below the knee, one can usually tie off veins with impunity. Damage to major veins above the knee may result in limb swelling and, if possible, one should attempt to reconstruct them. Both veins and arteries can be damaged during surgical procedures and early recognition and treatment is essential. Direct damage to the veins can also occur when bones are broken, following an assault in which the limb is stabbed, or following gunshot injuries.

CHAPTER 5

# INVESTIGATION OF ARTERIAL DISEASE

## INTRODUCTION

When investigating patients with arterial problems, the first and most important step is to consider the diagnosis. It is a failure to consider the possibility of arterial disease that leads to early management mistakes, with potentially disastrous long term problems.

As part of the investigation of patients with arterial problems, it is essential to take a full history. Once the history has been completed, a thorough clinical examination, first, of the area of complaint and, secondly, of the whole body, should be carried out. Having taken a history and completed a proper physical examination, a provisional diagnosis should be made. Sometimes it is not possible to make a precise diagnosis and a series of alternative diagnoses should be considered (differential diagnosis).

The purpose of an investigation is to confirm or amend a diagnosis. Care should be taken not to jump to premature conclusions or to proceed to complex and expensive investigations when simple investigations would suffice. Investigations themselves may be associated with complications and should therefore only be carried out when appropriate. If an investigation is associated with a significant complication, these problems should be explained to the patient in the same way that the problems associated with a surgical operation should be explained. The patient should be made aware of the need for the investigation, why this particular investigation needs to be carried out, what information will be obtained from the investigation and how that will affect their management, what complications can occur and, if they do occur, what treatment will be necessary.

It is important to remember that patients presenting with arterial disease in the legs may also have arterial disease affecting other systems, including the circulation to the heart, the brain, the kidneys and, indeed, any other organs. Having established the cause of the patient's problem, other potentially serious co-existing disease should be excluded. If the patient requires surgery, it will be necessary to establish their fitness to undergo the procedure and this will probably involve other tests.

# HISTORY

It is important to establish a proper history. This includes the nature of the patient's symptoms, their duration and what makes the symptoms better or worse. In a patient presenting with pain in the legs, a systematic inquiry should be made to exclude pain in the chest on exercise (angina), funny turns and visual disturbance (transient ischaemic attacks); inquiries should be made concerning past medical problems, including operations. Specific questions about whether the patient suffers from diabetes, heart disease and kidney disease should also be made. It is important to know whether patients are taking medication, as medication can affect symptoms of arterial disease (beta blockers given for heart disease can make intermittent claudication [pain in the legs] worse). A past history of thrombotic problems, deep vein thrombosis or pulmonary embolism should also be elicited. Some patients with arterial problems have a family history, with one or both parents suffering from similar problems. This information may also be useful. Smoking may adversely affect the symptoms and it is important to determine whether a patient smokes, the number they smoke and, in particular, whether they are trying to give up smoking. When taking a history, particularly with a patient with arterial disease, their job and home circumstances may be important. For example, patients with severe arterial disease may come to amputation. If this is recognised at an early stage, arrangements can be made to provide additional services or to re-house the patient. This may prevent a significant delay in hospital discharge.

# EXAMINATION

A physical examination of a patient with arterial disease can be carried out by any doctor. This includes general practitioners, junior hospital doctors and consultant vascular surgeons. Whilst it is important to record abnormal signs, it can be extremely helpful to record normal signs as well.

## Inspection

The first part of the examination involves inspection. This will involve undressing the patient and carrying out an examination in a well lit room. Inspection involves looking for the presence or absence of deformity, abnormalities of the skin, abnormalities of colour and the presence of scars.

## Palpation

Palpation involves feeling the skin and noting differences in temperature. As one moves from the groin to the foot, there will be a temperature drop. A comparison can be made between the right and left legs. Increased areas of temperature may suggest inflammation; decreased areas of temperature may suggest a reduced circulation. The pulses should be examined. When feeling for a pulse, one is feeling, first, whether the pulse is present or absent; secondly, whether it is weak or strong; thirdly, whether it is regular or irregular; and, finally, whether the artery feels hard or soft, in an attempt to determine the nature of the vessel wall. The best way to feel a pulse is to identify its position by using bony landmarks. If the doctor feels in the wrong place, then he will not know whether the pulse is absent because he is feeling in the wrong place or whether it is absent because the artery itself is blocked. A femoral pulse is felt at a point midway between the superior anterior iliac spine and the symphysis pubis. The popliteal pulse is felt in the midline immediately behind the knee. In most normal people, it is not possible to palpate this pulse. The presence of a readily palpable popliteal pulse may suggest aneurysmal dilatation of the artery. One would normally expect to palpate foot pulses – the dorsalis pedis pulse is felt on the front of the foot, while the posterior tibial pulse is felt immediately behind the medial malleolus. It is almost as important to record whether these pulses are present as it is to record that they are absent.

## Auscultation

Auscultation (listening with a stethoscope) will reveal turbulence. If there is narrowing in an artery, this causes turbulent flow and turbulent flow can be heard as a murmur. When carrying out a physical examination of a patient, one listens for turbulence over the femoral artery, the aorta above the umbilicus, the heart and over the carotid arteries in the neck. A murmur at the groin can be caused by turbulence arising in the lower aorta or iliac vessels. The presence of a murmur does not necessarily indicate arterial disease at the site where the murmur is heard. Murmurs travel out towards the edge of the body (distally) and indicate disease either at the site or more centrally. Murmurs arising from the heart can be transmitted into the neck and, occasionally, transmitted into the femoral artery. As part of the examination, it is necessary to record the blood pressure and to carry out an examination of the eyes using an ophthalmoscope (small emboli from the carotid arteries can produce abnormalities in the retina).

## ROUTINE TESTS

The following investigations will usually be carried out.:

(a) testing of haemoglobin levels: anaemia (reduced haemoglobin) reduces the oxygen carrying capacity of the blood and may precipitate symptoms of intermittent claudication;

(b) urea and electrolytes: an investigation used to carry out kidney function, which may be affected in arterial disease;

(c) chest X-ray to exclude underlying chest disease: many patients with arterial disease were heavy smokers;

(d) electrocardiogram (ECG): carried out to assess heart function, as cardiac disease often co-exists with arterial disease; and

(e) urine analysis: urine is checked to exclude diabetes.

## DOPPLER/ULTRASOUND STETHOSCOPE

The ultrasound stethoscope relies on the Doppler principle. Sound waves that hit a column of moving fluid are reflected back, but at a different frequency. This alteration in frequency (the Doppler shift) is audible and indicates blood flow. This instrument is particularly useful when a pulse may not be palpable, yet there is still blood flowing through the artery. A bi-directional Doppler ultrasound stethoscope will detect forward and backward flow. In normal healthy arteries, each heart beat is associated with a triphasic flow pattern. The loss of this triphasic pattern is one of the first signs of arterial disease. As the arteries become narrowed, the signal becomes more prolonged.

## ANKLE BRACHIAL PRESSURE INDEX

By placing a blood pressure cuff around the arm and inflating it whilst listening with a Doppler/ultrasound stethoscope, the brachial artery (arm) sounds disappear with inflation of the cuff, which occludes the artery. The pressure at which this occlusion takes place is known as the brachial pressure. If the same process is repeated by applying the blood pressure cuff around the calf (see Figure 5.1), the pressure at which either the posterior tibial or the dorsalis pedis artery disappears can also be noted. By expressing the ankle pressure over the brachial pressure a ratio is achieved. The normal ratio is 1:1. A ratio of less than this indicates arterial impairment.

# Investigation of Arterial Disease

**Figure 5.1**  Ankle Brachial Pressure Index

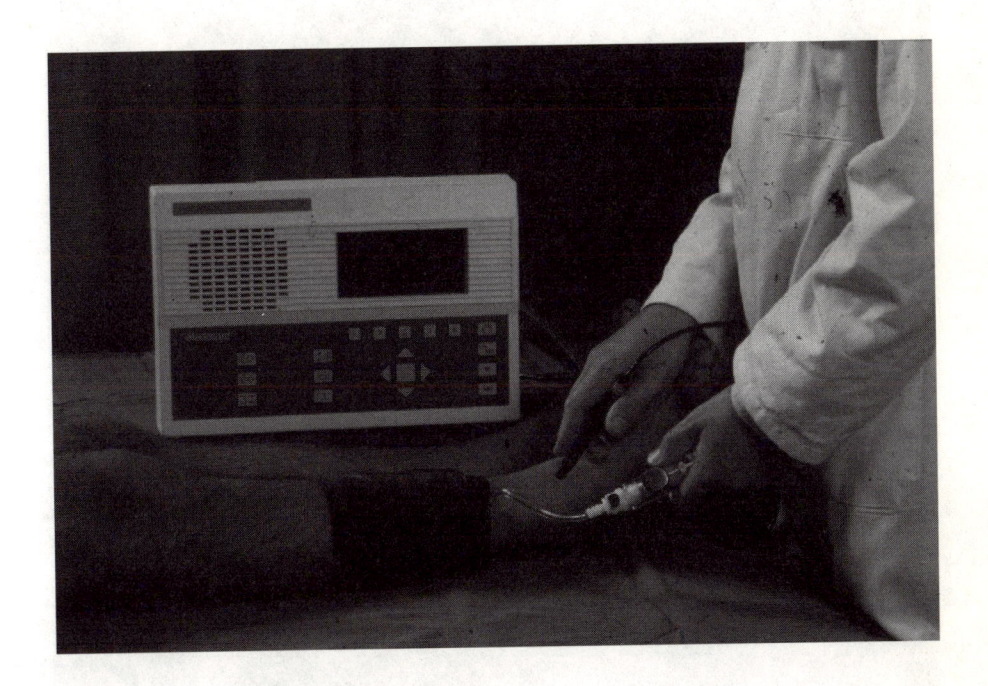

## DUPLEX ULTRASOUND IMAGING

Ultrasound is the biological equivalent of radar. A signal is reflected back whenever there is a change in the surface. These reflections are recorded and mapped, giving a cross-sectional profile. Duplex ultrasound imaging involves coupling a Doppler probe to an ultrasound machine (see Figure 5.2). By sampling a different depth, forward and backward flow can be determined. Flow can be coloured red or blue, depending on whether it is going forwards or backwards. This allows a complete map of the vessels to be constructed. The latest generation of duplex ultrasound machines allow extremely good visualisation of all the major arteries and provide useful information about the nature and volume of blood flowing through the arteries. Duplex ultrasound imaging provides both anatomical and physiological information about the arterial system. In many centres, duplex ultrasound imaging is beginning to replace arteriography as a diagnostic test. It does, however, depend on extremely skilled technologists or specially trained radiologists and vascular surgeons to carry out these procedures. The procedure itself is totally non-invasive.

Vascular Surgery

**Figure 5.2**  Duplex ultrasound machine

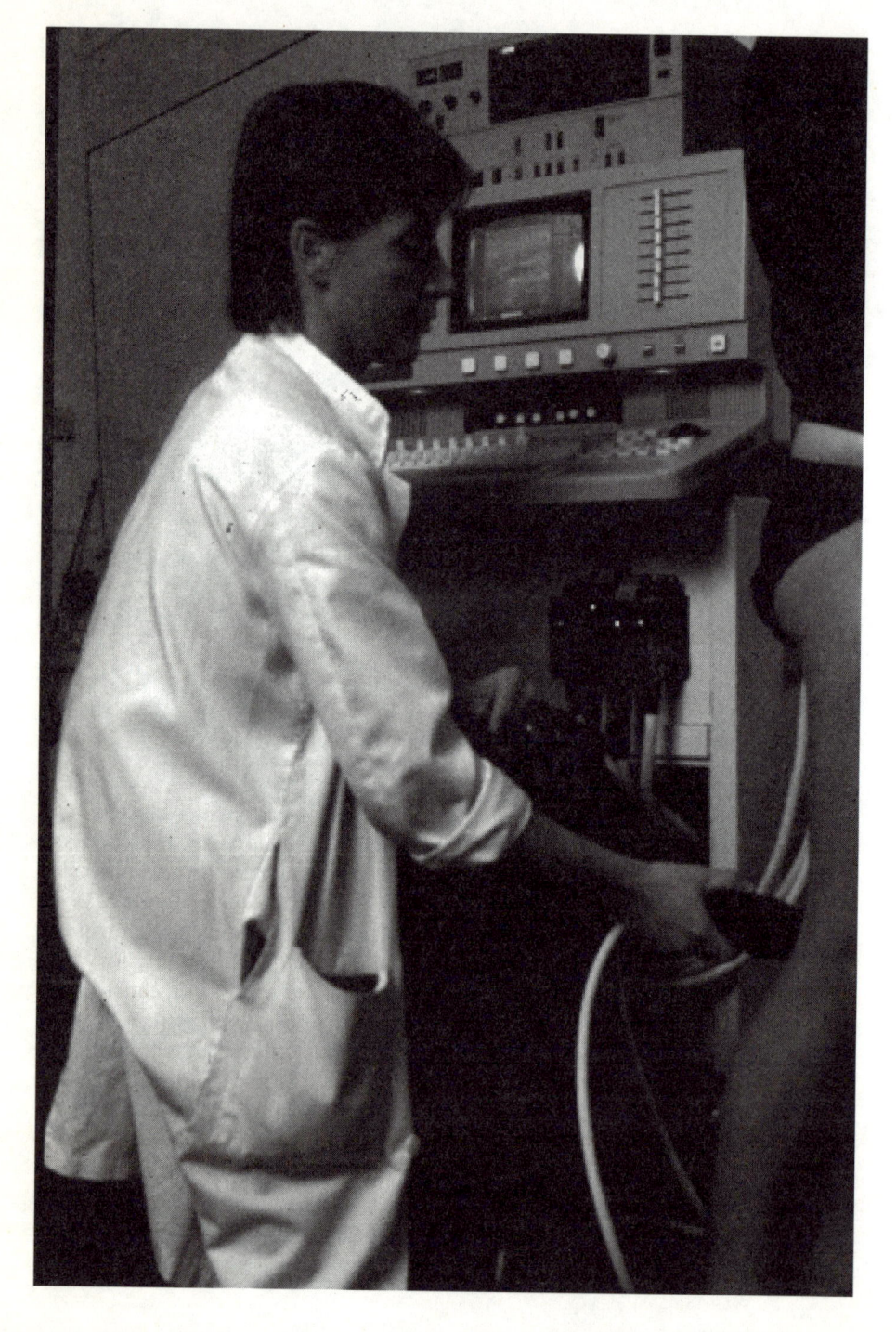

# Investigation of Arterial Disease

## ARTERIOGRAPHY

Arteriography involves the injection of dyes, which are radio opaque, into arteries. X-rays can then be taken, which outline the arterial tree (see Figures 5.4 and 5.5). Conventional arteriography involves inserting a needle into an artery and injecting the dye. The dye will flow down the artery and, therefore, an injection in the groin will only outline the vessels below the groin going towards the feet. If an outline of vessels nearer the heart is required, then, having inserted a needle into the artery, a fine guide wire is passed through the needle, the needle is withdrawn and a flexible catheter is inserted over the guide wire (Seldinger technique). This allows a fine catheter to be inserted higher up the arterial tree. The catheter can be advanced as far as the heart and indeed into the coronary arteries if necessary (selective arteriography). Once the injection has taken place, X-rays have to be taken in quick succession before the contrast material is washed out of the arterial system.

**Figure 5.3** **Arteriogram (Seldinger technique)**

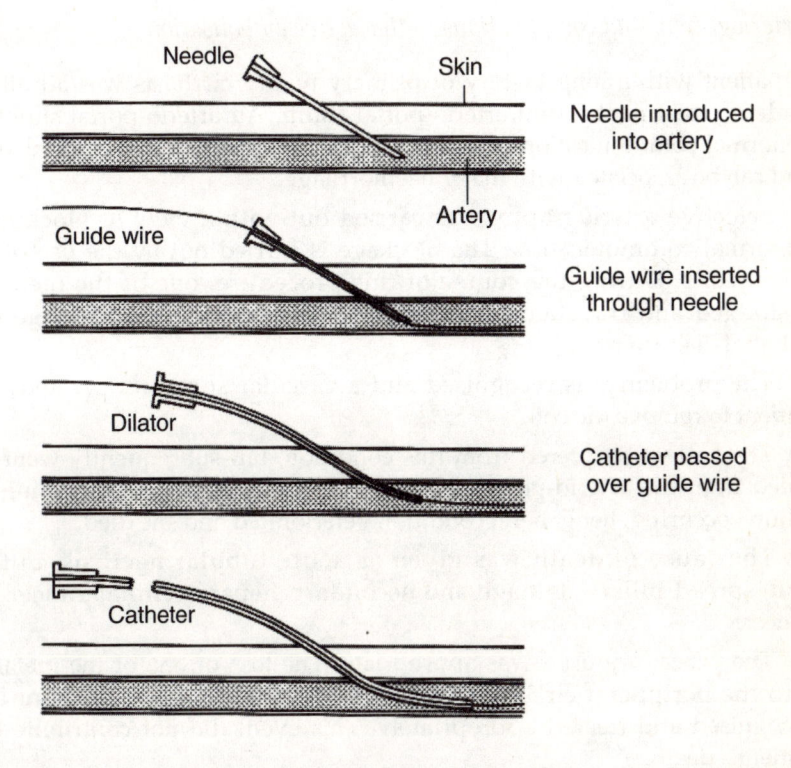

Needle introduced into artery

Guide wire inserted through needle

Catheter passed over guide wire

Note: the needle can damage the wall of the artery, leading to a dissection

Arteriography involves inserting needles into arteries. The arteries may be hardened and may have solid calcified plaques on their wall. When inserting a needle into an artery through one of these plaques, the plaque may become dislodged and embolise. Embolisation can then obstruct the flow of blood. This is a recognised complication and, if it happens, further treatment should be carried out as a matter of urgency. Sometimes the needle causes part of the arterial wall to separate, the arterial wall rolling down inside the artery to cause an obstruction (dissection). Injection of contrast material may be associated with allergic reactions and particularly sensitive patients should be tested before the procedure is carried out. In some instances, it is necessary to cover the procedure with the simultaneous administration of a steroid.

Before carrying out arteriography, it is important that the patient realises that this procedure may lead to circulatory problems and that further treatment may be needed.

*Case*

## Arteriography and complications with elective embolisation

A patient with a long history of primary biliary cirrhosis was admitted to undergo treatment for an arterio-portal shunt. An arterio-portal shunt is an abnormal communication between the arterial system and the portal system, and can be associated with major haemorrhage.

Selective arteriography was carried out with a view to blocking this abnormal communication. The blockage is carried out by the use of small metal coils. During the course of this procedure, one of the metal coils dislodged and travelled through the arterial circulation to lodge in the external iliac artery.

The problem was recognised and a vascular surgeon operated on the patient to remove the coil.

The patient recovered from this condition, but subsequently went on to bleed from the arterio-portal shunt. Further complications, including renal failure, occurred, her general condition deteriorated and she died.

The cause of death was given as acute tubular necrosis, but with widespread biliary damage and secondary hepato-cellular cancer (liver cancer).

The procedure used was appropriate. The loss of one of the metal coils into the peripheral circulation is a well recognised complication. It was recognised and treated appropriately. This event did not contribute to the patient's death.

Following medical reports, this case did not proceed.

Investigation of Arterial Disease

**Figure 5.4**  Arteriogram, showing aorto-iliac disease

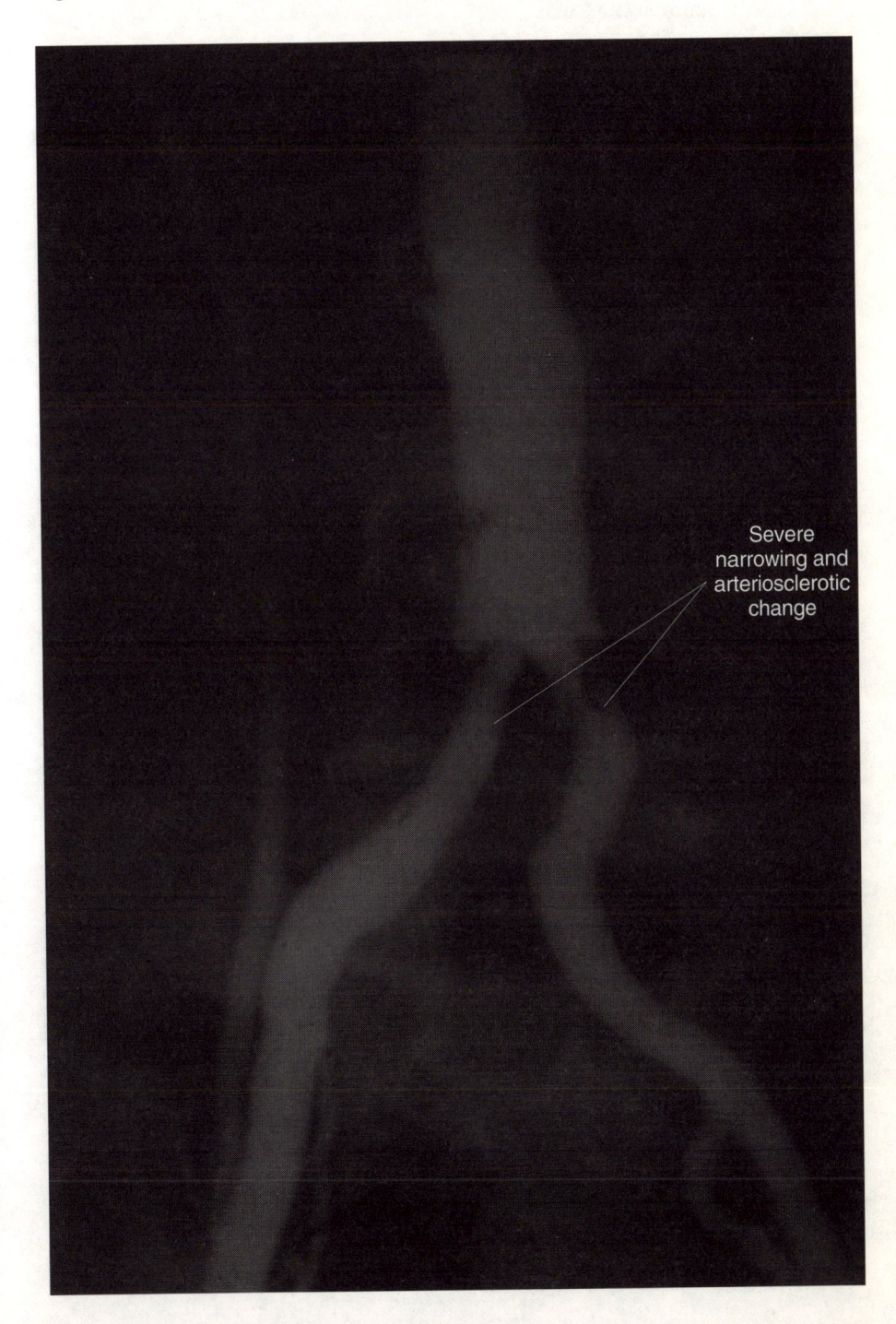

Vascular Surgery

**Figure 5.5** Arteriogram, showing superficial femoral artery occlusion above the knee

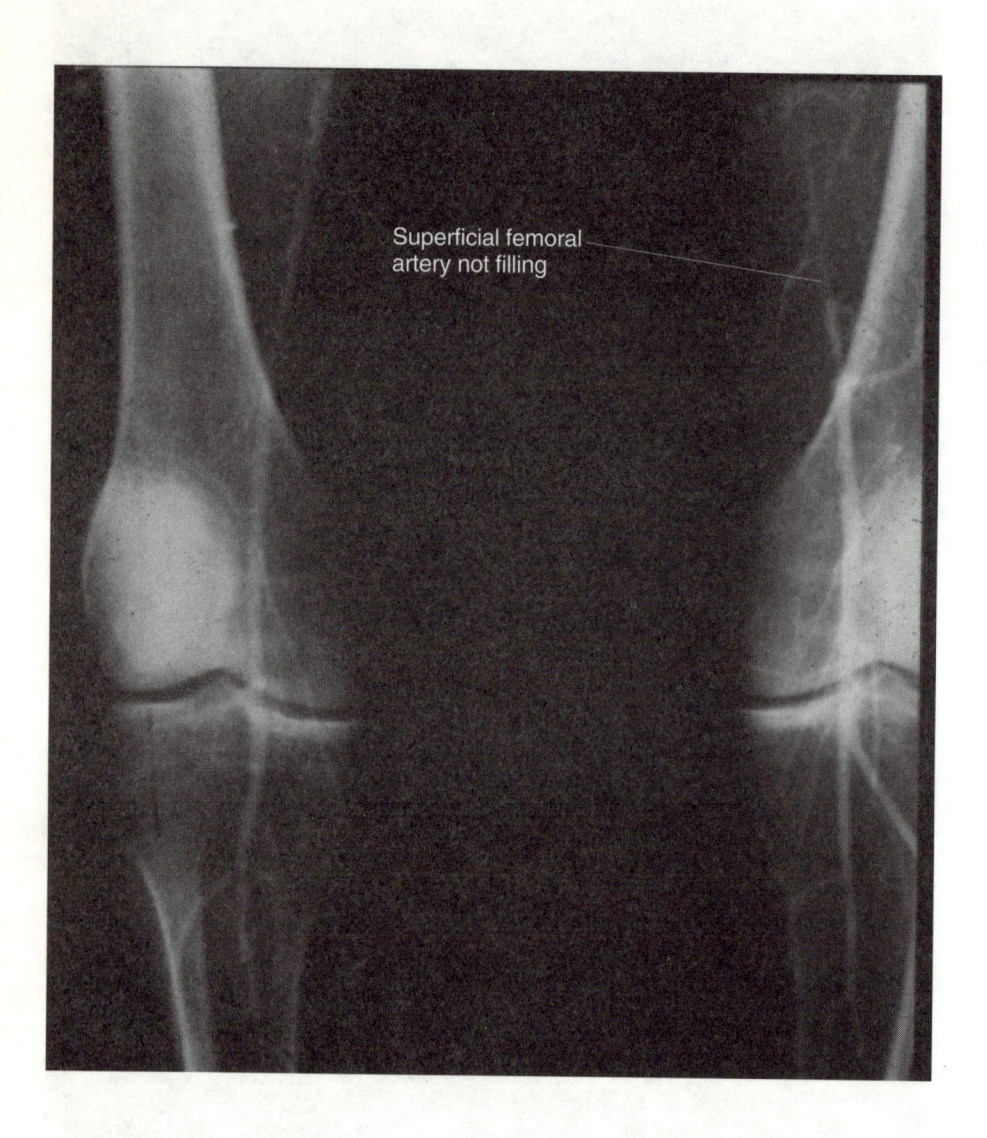

Investigation of Arterial Disease

## DIGITAL SUBTRACTION ANGIOGRAPHY

Digital subtraction angiography (DSA) involves computer enhancement to produce arterial images (see Figure 5.6a–d) from an intravenous injection or a very small intra-arterial injection. An X-ray picture is taken of a patient immediately prior to an injection of contrast material. The image is recorded on a computer in digital form. An intravenous injection of contrast material is given. This travels first to the heart, then through the lungs, before being pumped through the arterial system. The contrast material will eventually be cleared but, prior to this, it becomes distributed, first throughout the whole arterial system and then throughout the arterial and venous system. If a further X-ray picture is taken to coincide with the contrast material arriving in the arterial circulation (a few seconds after injection), then this picture can be stored in the computer too. If the computer then subtracts the first image from the second image, all that is left is the contrast material, the contrast material being the only difference between the first and the second image. It is then possible to enhance this image, giving an outline of the arterial tree. The resolution is very good and may avoid the need for a direct arterial puncture. If particularly good quality images are required, then a small intra-arterial injection using a fine needle and a small volume of contrast material will achieve this. All arteries in the body, including those in the lungs and the brain, can be imaged in this way.

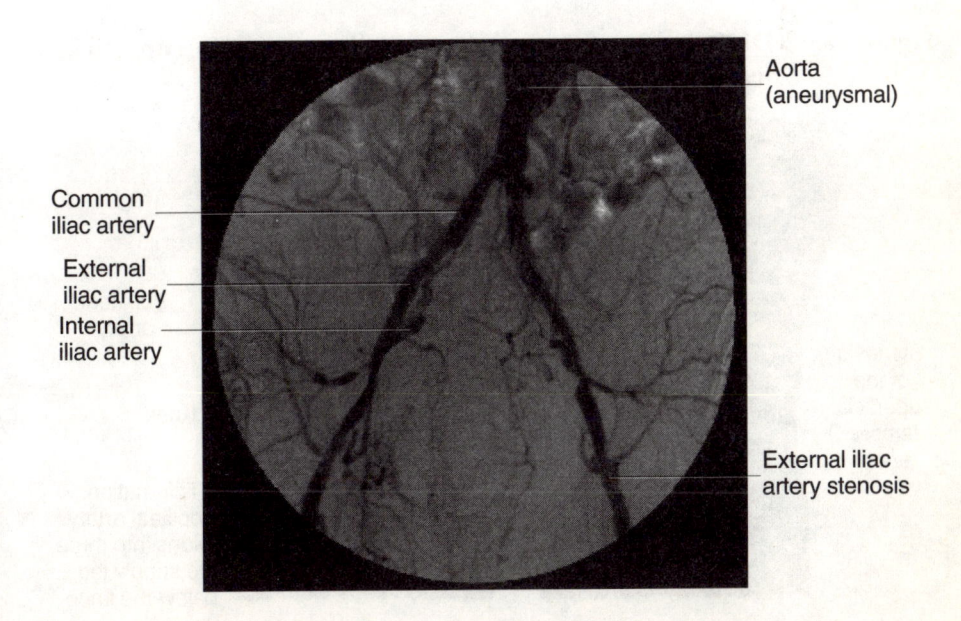

**Figure 5.6a**     **Digital subtraction angiogram, showing aorto-iliac vessels**

**Figure 5.6b** Digital subtraction angiogram, showing vessels of the left leg

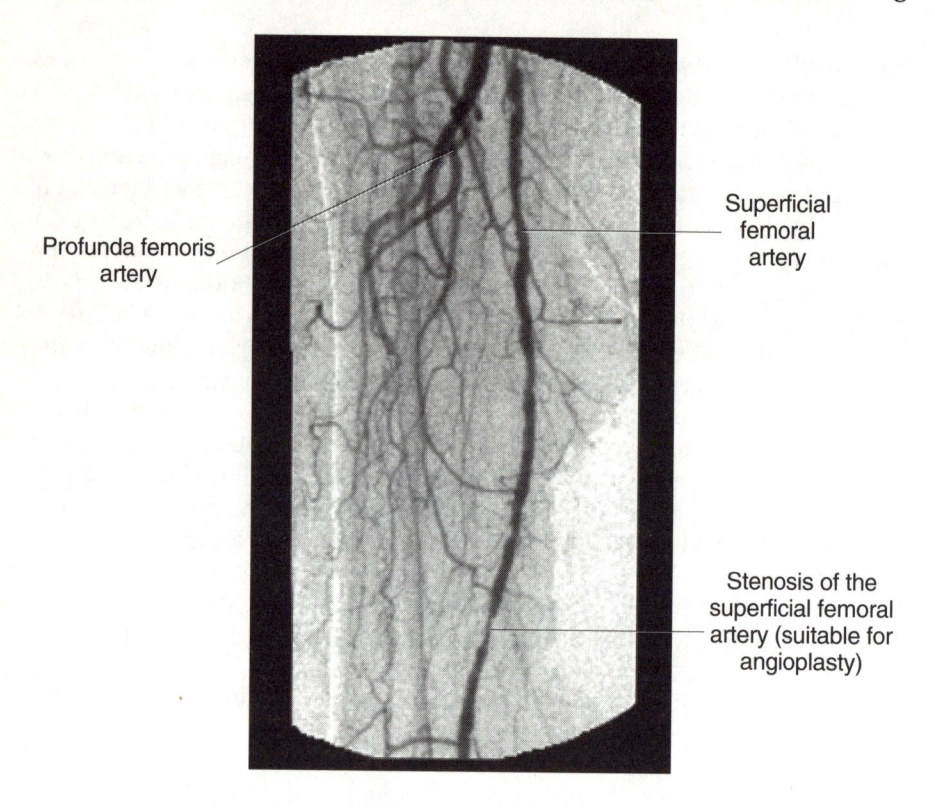

**Figure 5.6c** Digital subtraction angiogram, showing both superficial femoral vessels

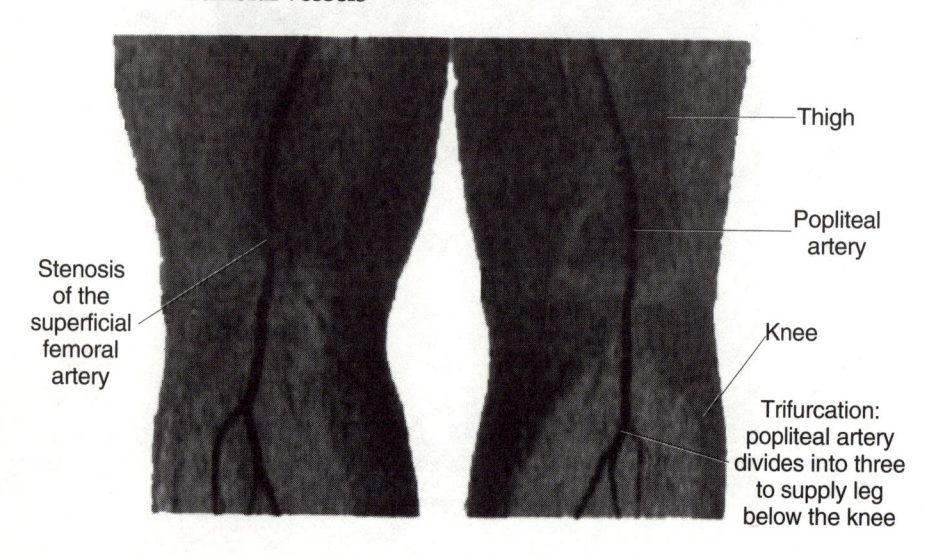

**Figure 5.6d** Digital subtraction angiogram, showing popliteal artery

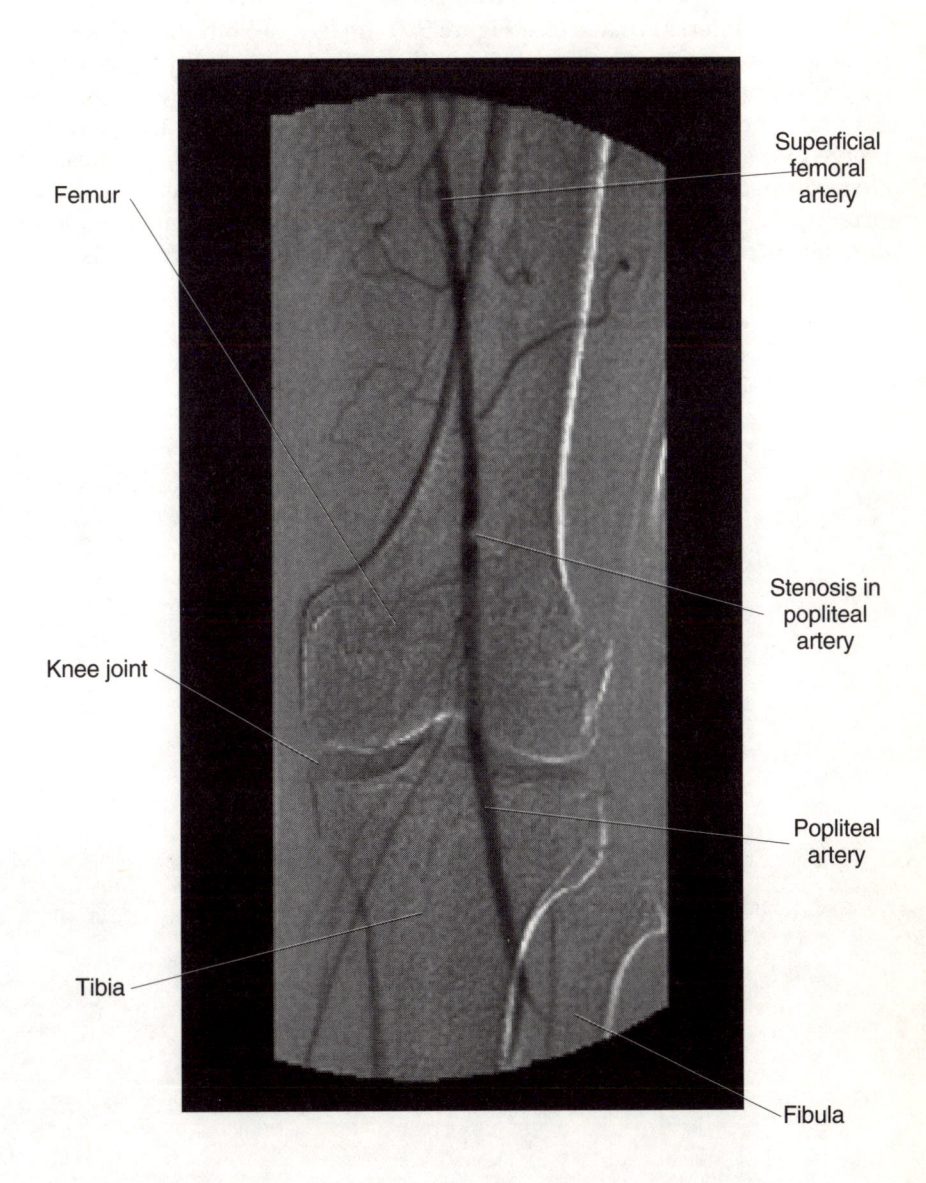

## MAGNETIC RESONANCE IMAGING

Magnetic resonance imaging (MRI) relies on resonance induced in a strong magnetic field. Different tissues will resonate at different frequencies, producing a different image (see Figure 5.7). Images of both the venous and the arterial system can be produced with outstanding quality without the need for any intravenous intra-arterial injections or the use of contrast material. These investigations are slow and expensive and are currently reserved for specific indications. Sensitivity to contrast material, the presence of co-existing renal failure and the investigation of the cerebral circulation are currently the principal indications. Magnetic resonance imaging would not normally be carried out for the assessment of straightforward arterial disease.

Investigation of Arterial Disease

**Figure 5.7    MRI arteriograms**

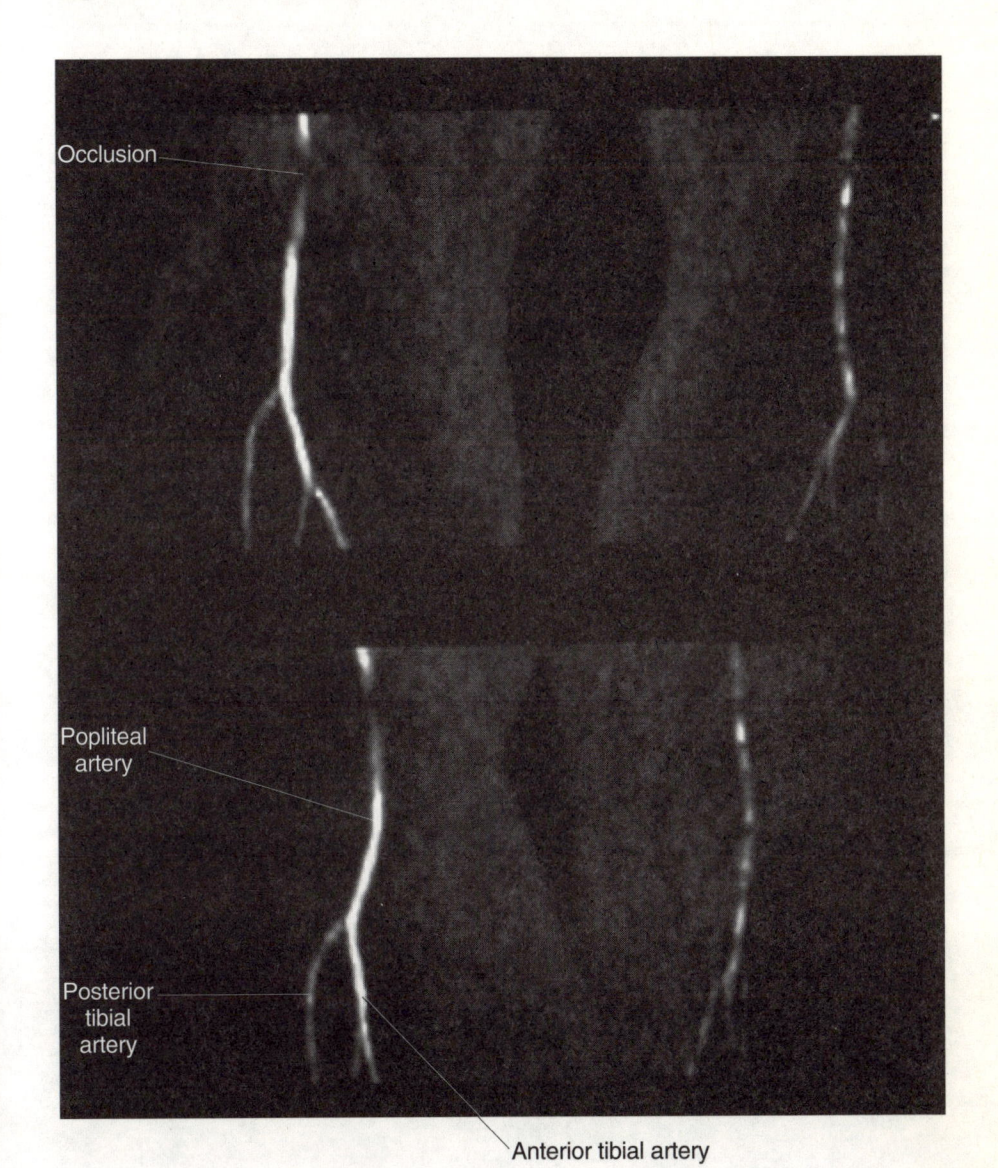

CHAPTER 6

# TREATMENT OF ARTERIAL DISEASE I

## INTRODUCTION

Arteriosclerotic disease is a condition where the artery hardens and narrows. Before carrying out any treatment, it is important to assess the patient properly to determine the extent of the arterial disease and whether there is any co-existing medical condition which may be affected by treating the arterial problem; it is then necessary to decide whether the treatment is really indicated. A patient presenting with intermittent claudication (pain in the calves) after walking half a mile would not normally be a candidate for surgical treatment. He would normally be advised to exercise, to walk into the pain, as this will stimulate the opening up of new vessels, to stop smoking and to come back if his condition deteriorates. He would also be told to report immediately to the accident and emergency department if he notices any sudden changes in the colour of his leg, or presents with severe pain. In some patients, operating on them may improve their claudication only to reveal an underlying problem with their heart (angina). There are no absolute rules as to who gets operated on and who does not, but careful attention should be paid to each individual patient's lifestyle. If a patient's quality of life is suffering as a result of severe arterial disease, then one might be inclined to operate at an earlier stage. It should be remembered that, even in the best hands, arterial surgery is unpredictable, and that embarking upon one operation may lead in rapid succession to a series of operations, culminating in the loss of a limb.

## Management of a patient with intermittent claudication (arterial insufficiency in the legs)

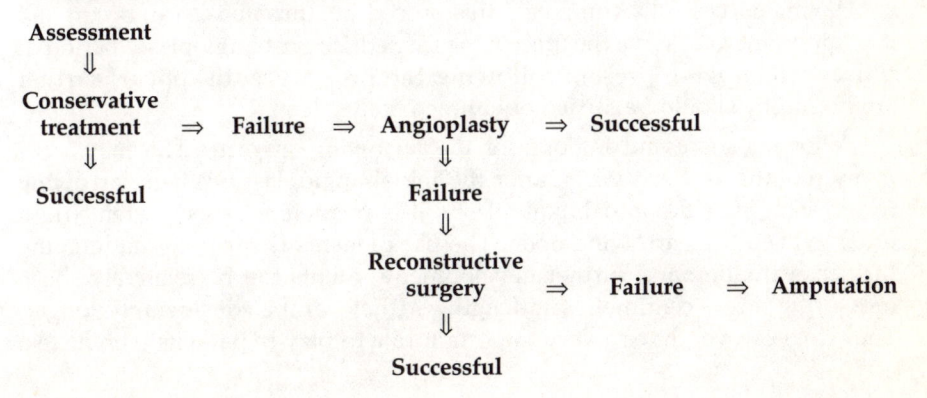

Assessment
⇓
Conservative
treatment ⇒ Failure ⇒ Angioplasty ⇒ Successful
⇓ ⇓
Successful Failure
⇓
Reconstructive
surgery ⇒ Failure ⇒ Amputation
⇓
Successful

# ANGIOPLASTY

Angioplasty is a technique which involves stretching an artery to open up narrowed segments to improve the flow of blood through it. This procedure should only be embarked upon after careful patient assessment, as complications and failure may lead to further surgical procedures and possibly the loss of a limb. The procedure itself is very much simpler than a major surgical intervention and eminently suitable for use in elderly patients who would not have been considered for surgical treatment. It is often combined with arteriography and, in many units, patients are prepared to undergo angioplasty at the same time as undergoing the initial arteriography. When a patient has a narrowing of an artery or a very short occlusion of the artery it should be possible, initially, to pass a guide wire and, secondly, a catheter through this segment (see Figure 6.1). Having confirmed that the catheter is still within the lumen of the artery, the catheter can be replaced by a special catheter with a balloon on the end of it. The catheter is introduced such that the balloon extends from the top of the narrowing to the bottom of the narrowing. Once the balloon is in the correct position, it is inflated with saline for a period of one minute (see Figure 6.3). The balloon is then released, before being re-inflated two or three times. The effect of inflating the balloon in a narrowed segment is to compress the obstructing material back into the arterial wall. At the end of the procedure, a further injection of dye is given, to check that the lumen of the artery is now patent (open).

This procedure can be associated with a number of complications. It may not be possible to insert the balloon into the correct position and the procedure may need to be abandoned. Having inserted the balloon into the correct position, damage to the wall may occur, such that part of the lining will roll down, causing a total obstruction of the artery. Under these circumstances, it is usually necessary to explore the artery to remove that part of the lining and/or to reconstruct circulation to the legs. Catheters may become lodged and direct surgical exploration may be required to remove them.

Having successfully completed this procedure, thrombosis can occur, and it is important to observe the limb in the immediate post-angioplasty period. If pulses which were present following the procedure disappear, further arteriography should be carried out immediately.

Following successful angioplasty, the narrowing can recur. This may occur many months, or even years, after the initial angioplasty. When narrowing recurs soon after the initial angioplasty, it is possible to insert a stent (rigid tube) to keep the narrowing open. The use of stents is currently undergoing further evaluation and further developments. Stents can be relatively short, measuring a few centimetres in length, or they can be considerably longer. They do, however, have a very important role to play in patients who have a narrow segment, which would normally be considered suitable for angioplasty, but where, for some reason, angioplasty fails to maintain a reasonable lumen.

**Figure 6.1    Percutaneous transluminal angioplasty**

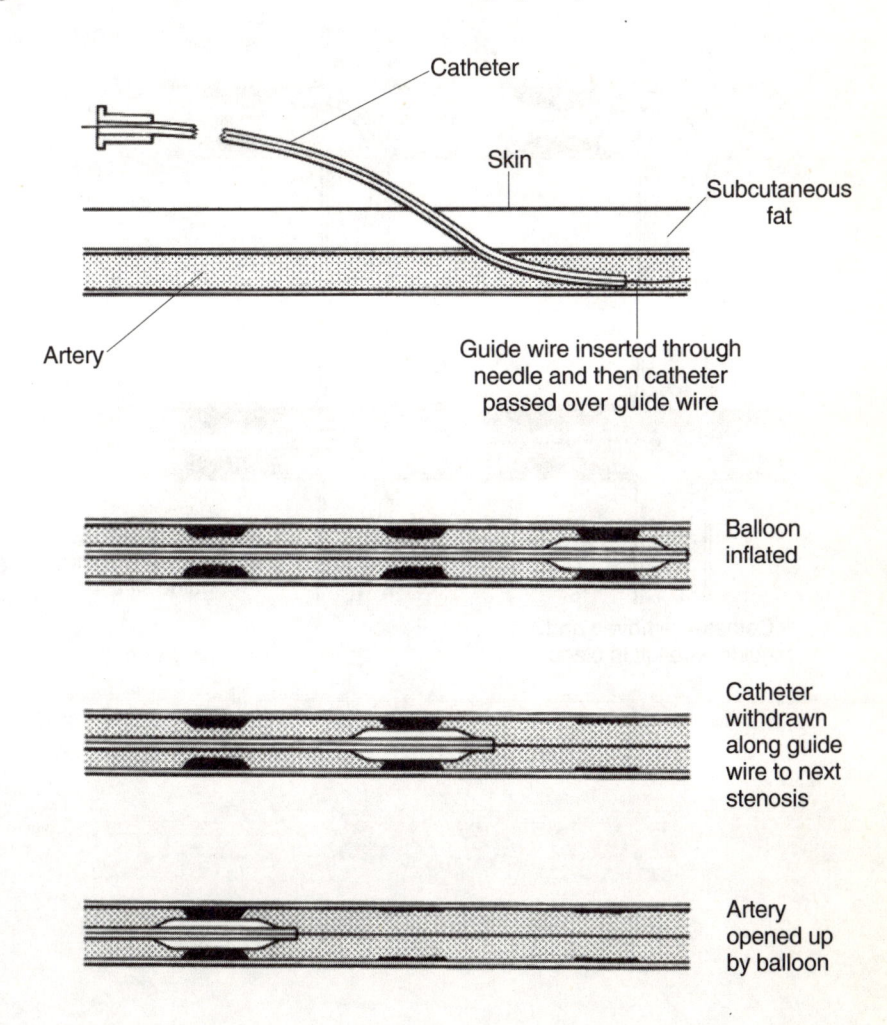

*Catheter*

*Skin*

*Subcutaneous fat*

*Artery*

Guide wire inserted through needle and then catheter passed over guide wire

Balloon inflated

Catheter withdrawn along guide wire to next stenosis

Artery opened up by balloon

Note: over inflation of the balloon may cause rupture of the artery

**Figure 6.2** **Selective catheterisation**

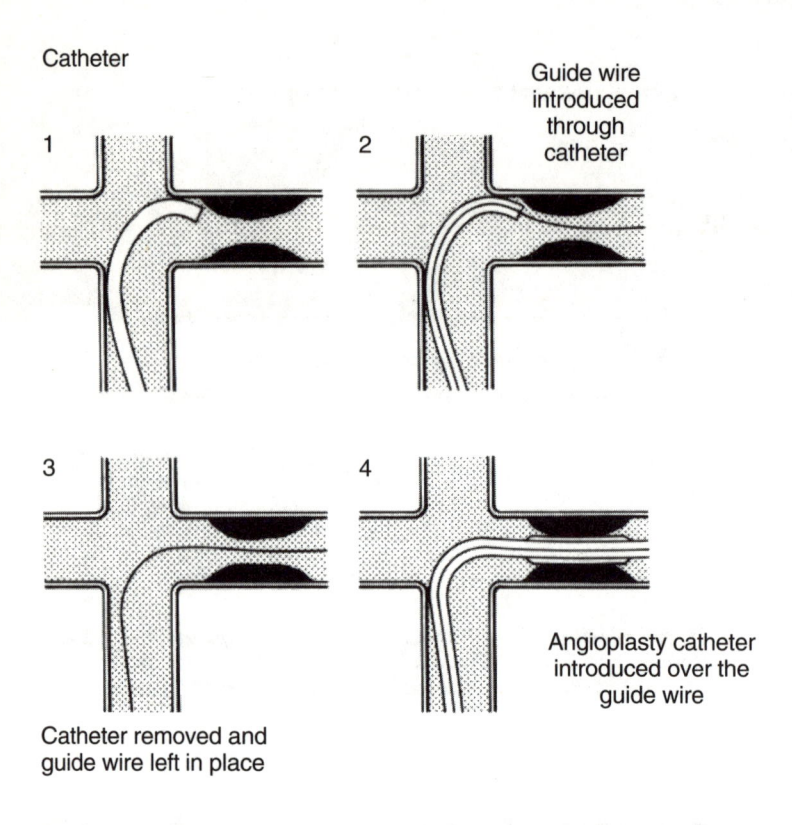

1. Catheter
2. Guide wire introduced through catheter
3. Catheter removed and guide wire left in place
4. Angioplasty catheter introduced over the guide wire

**Figure 6.3** **Technique of balloon inflation**

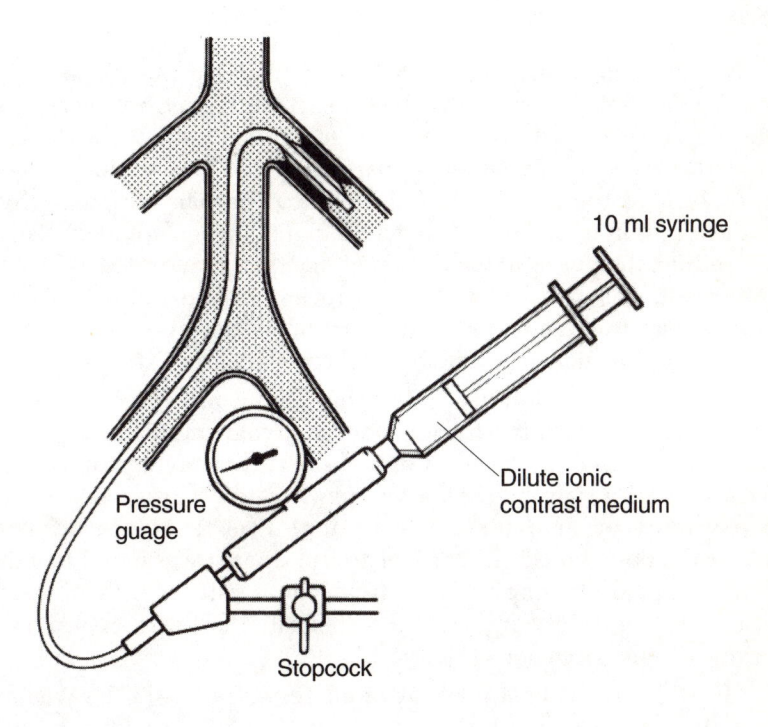

## Case

### Brachial artery injury following cardiac catheterisation (I)

A middle aged man was admitted to hospital. He was diagnosed as having myocardial infarction, from which he made a good recovery, and he was discharged. Following review in medical out-patients, a stress ECG was undertaken, which showed minimal changes. With a strong family history, it was decided the patient should undergo coronary angiography. Cardiac catheterisation was undertaken via the right brachial approach. Following the procedure, the pulses in the right arm/hand were recorded as being faint, but the patient was discharged following review with an out-patient appointment following an exercise test. The cardiac catheterisation showed normal ventricular function and double vessel coronary artery disease.

He was reviewed in the cardiac clinic and it was noted that his right hand was severely ischaemic. The right hand was cold and pulseless, and an arterial assessment was undertaken. A digital subtraction angiogram was performed. This showed a right brachial artery block with occlusion of the radial artery but patent ulnar artery. The patient was therefore admitted for a reconstruction of the right brachial artery, when it was found that the brachial artery appeared completely occluded by a suture. A thrombectomy was performed, and three inches of the brachial artery was excised and replaced with a reverse saphenous vein graft.

Post-operatively, the right hand remained pale; he was started on intravenous heparin but with no further improvement, so a further arteriogram was done, which showed a complete block of the right axillary artery. He therefore underwent re-exploration of the right atrial artery with thrombectomy and replacement of the main graft was carried out under general anaesthetic. Despite this procedure, the patient's hands remained cold, though the brachial pulse was palpable but weak. The patient remained heparinised and was gradually converted to warfarin.

On surgical review, it was noted that there was no change in the patient's symptoms and that his right arm was, in fact, painful, with hypoaesthesia and no grip. A further arteriogram was therefore arranged as an in-patient. This again demonstrated occlusion of the right axillary artery. However, the procedure was abandoned when the patient complained of headache and dysarthria. Following the arteriogram, the patient remained drowsy, with slurred speech which persisted for 24 hours, and it was felt that this was probably an embolic phenomenon secondary to the arteriogram. A neurological opinion was sought, which concluded that the patient had a pseudobulbar palsy secondary to embolism and that he had a high brain stem infarct. He was transferred to hospital for further investigations, where a CT (computerised tomography) scan confirmed the lesion.

Over the course of the following few days, the patient's condition continued to deteriorate and it became apparent that he had lost the use of all his limbs and could only communicate by blinking his eyes. Elective tracheostomy was undertaken and he was transferred back to hospital, where he continued to have numerous problems, including recurrent respiratory tract infections, and he was transferred to a hospital home, where he has remained since.

The plaintiff's case was that the arterial injury occurred at the time of brachial artery catheterisation. This should have been recognised and, if a vascular opinion had been sought, he would have undergone surgical exploration at that point, restoring the circulation in full to his arms.

As a result of failing to restore the circulation, he presented late with signs of arterial insufficiency to the limb, necessitating further investigation. This investigation would have been unnecessary at the time of the original injury. The investigation caused embolisation to the brain, resulting in the locked-in syndrome.

The defendant's case was that there was no evidence of arterial insufficiency at the end of the procedure and that, even if there had been, the vascular surgeon would not, at that stage, have undertaken surgery.

The plaintiff's experts argued that there would have been signs and symptoms that would have resulted in the vascular surgeon carrying out an immediate surgical reconstruction.

The defendant's arterial surgeon maintained his view that he would have done nothing if he had been asked to see the patient.

The judge found in favour of the defendants, referring to *Bolitho v City and Hackney Health Authority* [1993] 4 Med LR 381. The case was appealed on behalf of the plaintiff, but the original judgment was upheld.

*Case*

### Brachial artery injury following cardiac catheterisation (II)

A 35 year old man with suspected angina was referred by his general practitioner to a consultant cardiologist. He was reviewed by the cardiologist, who agreed that his history was suggestive of angina, and arranged his admission for a coronary angiogram. The patient was admitted to hospital for this, the operation being performed the following day by a registrar, assisted by a research registrar. There appear to have been problems gaining access to the right brachial artery during this procedure and bleeding from the artery when the wound was initially closed. At the end of the procedure, it was noted that no pulse was palpable, though a pulse was audible on a Doppler stethoscope, this showing a pressure drop of 30 mm Hg. Arrangements were made to refer the patient to the on-call cardiothoracic surgical team, although there is no record that the patient was reviewed by them. He was kept on the ward overnight and allowed home the following day. At no stage did his pulse become palpable, though it remained audible on Doppler.

Two weeks later, the patient's general practitioner noted that he had had a large haematoma following the cardiac catheterisation, which had now mostly resolved but had left the muscles of the forearm very tense and painful. The patient was reviewed by a consultant surgeon, who noted that he required reconstruction of the right brachial artery. A subclavian arteriogram was performed, confirming blockage of the brachial artery, and the consultant surgeon performed a reversed vein bypass graft. This was apparently initially successful, but the patient developed a wound infection and the graft subsequently thrombosed. This has left the patient with continuing ischaemia of the right arm, preventing him from carrying out many normal activities, though the consultant surgeon noted that this was still an improvement on his pre-operative condition.

Injury to the brachial artery following cardiac catheterisation is a well recognised complication. Because this complication can lead to pain in the arm and, indeed, may result in loss of an arm, most cardiologists now prefer a femoral approach.

The decision, however, to proceed to coronary angiography via the brachial artery can be defended, given that a recognised body of medical opinion use the same approach.

At the end of the procedure, there was clearly a problem with bleeding. This problem was recognised.

When he was reviewed, the limb was thought to be viable and a decision was made not to explore the artery.

When it became clear that there was a problem with the artery, he underwent an attempt at reconstruction. Despite carrying out a reconstruction, the result was poor.

It is probable that, if reconstruction had been carried out shortly after the time of injury, the outcome would have been better.

It was accepted that vascular injuries can occur following cardiac catheterisation. The delay in making the diagnosis probably did affect the outcome. This case was settled with a payment of £8,000 plus £4,000 in costs.

# ENDARTERECTOMY

This involves the removal of part of the lining of the arterial wall. Thirty years ago, this was a widely practised procedure. It involved removing the inner lining of the artery, opening up the lumen. Unfortunately, removal of the lining of the artery over a long length results in increased thrombogenicity of the arterial wall and progressive occlusion of the artery. This procedure is now reserved for a few specific indications. One of these indications includes narrowing of the carotid artery at the origin of the internal carotid artery. Here, a localised narrowing of the artery in the form of an eccentric plaque may give rise to embolic phenomena. The centre of the plaque ulcerates, blood adheres to this and breaks off, travelling to the brain, giving mini-strokes. Surgical intervention, with removal of this plaque, can prevent this problem from occurring and prevent a major stroke happening.

## Carotid arterial disease

Carotid arterial disease usually presents with transient ischaemic attacks. These may involve abnormalities of vision, transient blindness or minor stroke-like symptoms, with weakness and numbness occurring for short periods of time. By definition, a transient ischaemic attack is over within 24 hours. Patients presenting with these symptoms should be investigated for underlying carotid arterial disease. Some patients have no signs of cerebrovascular disease but, during the course of investigations for other medical problems, are noted to have narrowing of the carotid artery. There has been much debate as to whether to operate on asymptomatic patients with carotid artery stenosis. In the UK, the majority of surgeons will only operate on patients who are symptomatic. A recent study, however, has suggested that patients with a greater than 75% narrowing of the carotid artery should undergo surgery, as they are at an increased risk of having a stroke. Patients with carotid artery disease run the risk of a 2% per annum incidence of stroke.

Non-surgical treatment of carotid artery disease involves the use of anti-platelet agents (aspirin). The use of anticoagulants (warfarin) is common practice but the evidence of the benefit of this does not exist.

Prior to carrying out carotid artery surgery, the patient should be fully assessed. In many centres, a neurological opinion forms part of this assessment.

In those patients where surgery is considered appropriate, the patient must be warned of the risk of stroke. Carotid artery surgery is associated with a 1% incidence of stroke. The operation involves a dissection high in the neck and there are many important nerves running through this region, including nerves to the tongue and face (see Figure 6.4a). It is normal practice to warn patients about potential nerve damage, although, in reality, the risk of damage

## Vascular Surgery

causing significant symptoms is quite low and, certainly, should be less than 1%. There is, however, a risk of a stroke occurring, even after apparently successful surgery. All patients undergoing carotid surgery should be warned of this risk. The risk of undergoing surgery should always be less than the risk of not undergoing surgery.

The operation itself is carried out under general anaesthetic. The artery is exposed and clamps are placed to isolate the bifurcation of the carotid artery. The carotid artery can then be opened and the atheromatous plaque removed (see Figure 6.4b). This procedure usually takes less than 10 minutes and can, in most patients, be carried out quite safely without the use of a temporary bypass (shunt). If the circulation through the other carotid artery is severely compromised, then shunting is probably advisable. A shunt involves the insertion of one end of a plastic tube into the common carotid artery; the other end is then inserted into the internal carotid artery. Once the atheromatous plaque has been removed, the incision in the artery can be closed. The shunt is removed before the final sutures are inserted. Following the procedure, the patient should be carefully monitored and, if there is any evidence of neurological abnormalities, further exploration of the carotid artery should be undertaken. This may be preceded by either a duplex ultrasound assessment or arteriography, depending on the unit.

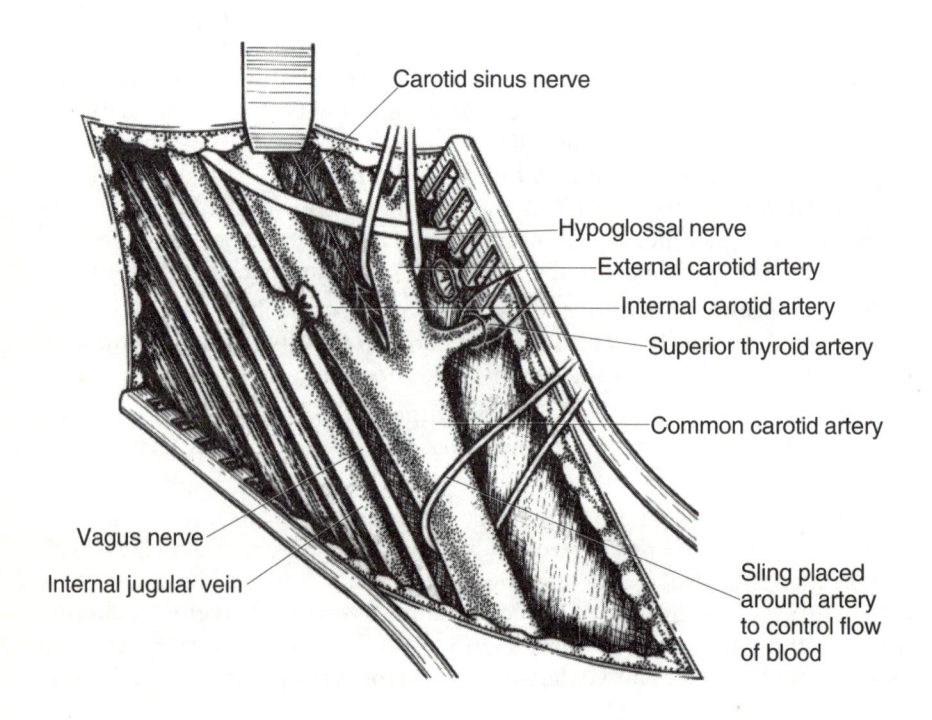

Figure 6.4a     Carotid endarterectomy

**Figure 6.4b**   Carotid endarterectomy: removal of atheromatous plaque

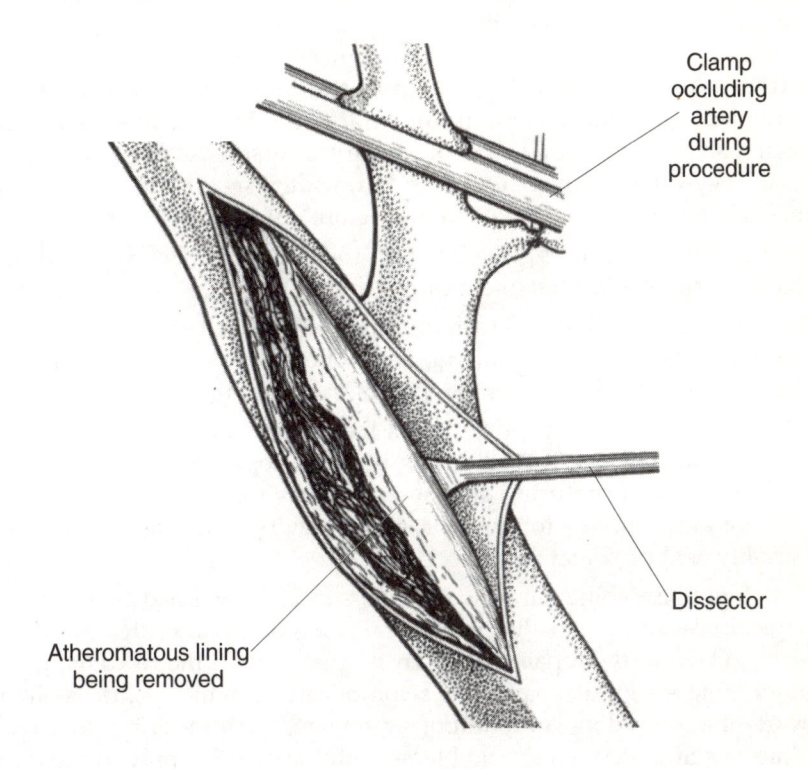

## AORTIC ANEURYSM

Arteries weakened by arteriosclerotic disease may dilate rather than stenose. An artery dilating is very similar to a balloon being inflated. As the balloon enlarges, the wall thins until it finally bursts. The incidence of aortic aneurysm increases with age. The diagnosis may be made by routine examination for an unrelated problem. A normal aorta in a man is 2.5 cm in diameter; aneurysms of greater than 5 cm are at risk of rupturing, though rupture of an aneurysm of less than 5 cm can occur. The best results are achieved when the diagnosis is made before the aneurysm leaks or ruptures. This depends on the diagnosis being made either by clinical examination or by an ultrasound examination. Any patient with an aortic aneurysm of less than 5 cm should undergo repeat scanning of the aorta. If the aneurysm is increasing in size, surgical treatment should be carried out. Patients presenting with aneurysms greater than 5 cm are usually advised to undergo repair of the aneurysm.

Because of the high death rate following a rupture of a symptomless aortic aneurysm, screening is now being advised. Men over the age of 55 years with a family history of arterial disease can undergo an ultrasound scan.

The aorta is located at the back of the abdomen and covered by a peritoneal covering. If the aneurysm begins to leak, the peritoneal covering may contain the blood with the patient complaining of abdominal pain and, in particular, loin pain. The differential diagnosis is often one of renal colic. Any patient who is known to have an aortic aneurysm who complains of abdominal pain and has a fainting attack should be considered to have a leaking aortic aneurysm. When the aneurysm first leaks, the patient may feel faint. They often recover from this and, if they seek medical attention, can undergo repair of the aortic aneurysm before full rupture occurs.

If a patient ruptures his aorta into the abdominal cavity, death usually occurs before medical treatment can be sought.

If a patient is known to have an aortic aneurysm, they should be investigated; they should undergo a pre-operative assessment to assess their cardiac status and then undergo repair of the aortic aneurysm.

Repair of an aortic aneurysm is a major surgical procedure. The patient should be aware that, if they do not undergo repair of the aortic aneurysm, they are at risk of rupturing their aorta. Surgery for a ruptured aorta carries a 40% mortality. Surgery for the repair of an aneurysm before ruptures carries a mortality of approximately 1%.

Before undergoing surgery, patients should be warned that it is a major surgical procedure and that it does carry a small risk of death. The risk of death following the repair, however, is smaller than the risk entailed in not undergoing surgical repair. Other complications which patients should be aware of are bleeding complications, problems with restoring the circulation to the legs and, very rarely, problems with the blood supply to organs in the abdominal cavity and blood supply to the spinal cord. Failure to establish a blood supply to abdominal organs or the spinal cord is unpredictable but, fortunately, a very rare event.

The operation (see Figure 6.5a–c) is carried out under general anaesthetic. It involves opening the abdomen and, sometimes, making separate incisions in the groin. The aorta is exposed at the back of the abdomen and a clamp is placed across the aorta above the aneurysm. Clamps are then placed on the iliac arteries below the aneurysm. The aneurysm is opened by incising it along its length. A woven dacron graft is then sewn into the aorta at the top of the aneurysm and into the aorta at the bottom of the aneurysm. If the aneurysm extends into the iliac arteries, a trouser-shaped graft is used, the legs of the trousers being inserted into the femoral arteries. Once the graft is sutured into place, the wall of the aortic aneurysm is then sutured across the top of the graft. At the end of the surgical procedure, it is important to establish that the circulation has been returned to the legs. Sometimes, following this procedure, the blood supply to one or other legs may not have returned and further surgical intervention may be required.

Treatment of Arterial Disease I

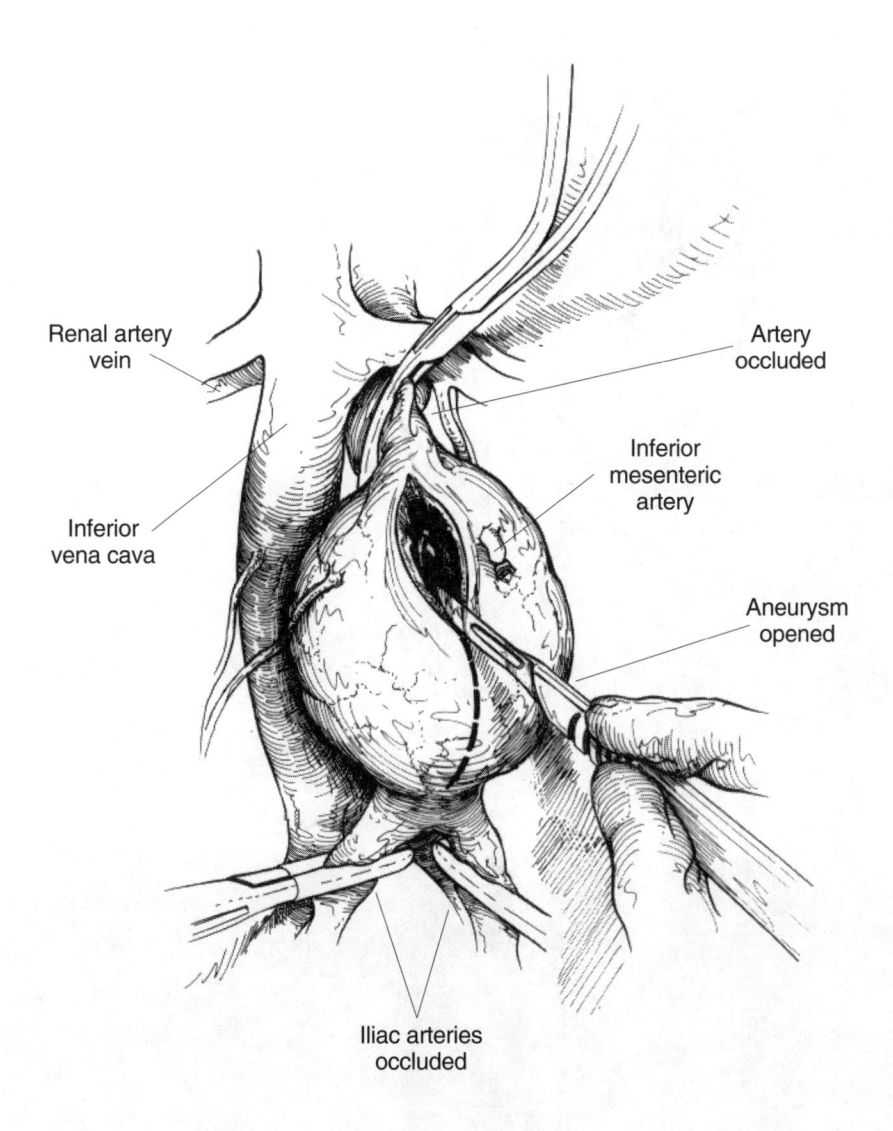

**Figure 6.5a** **Abdominal aortic aneurysm**

Vascular Surgery

**Figure 6.5b    Abdominal aortic aneurysm**

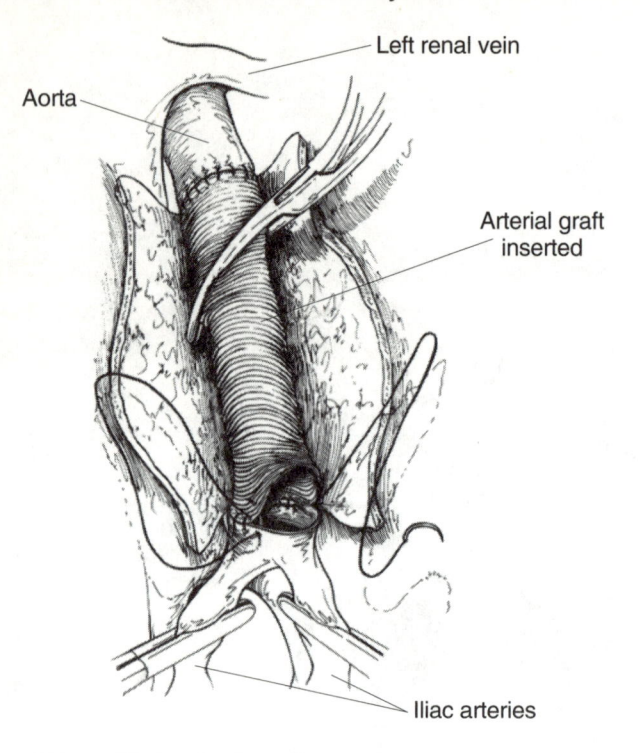

**Figure 6.5c    Abdominal aortic aneurysm**

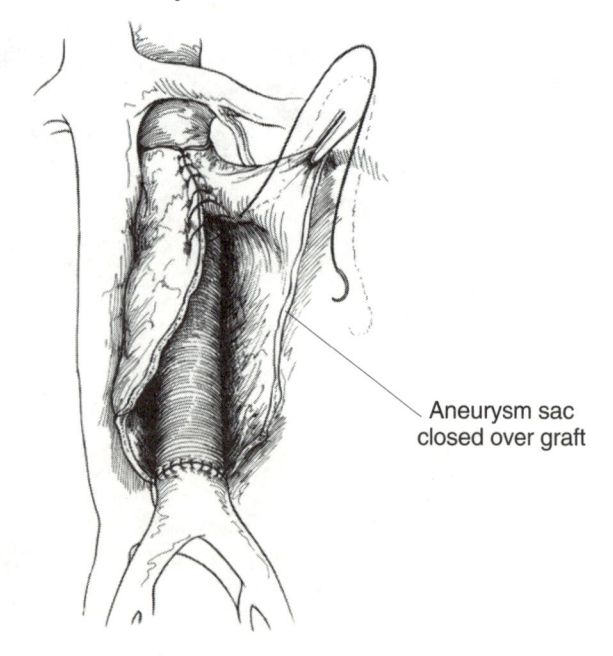

# BYPASS SURGERY

## Aorto-iliac disease

Blockage of the aorta or iliac arteries can be treated by bypass surgery. Early diagnosis can lead to treatment by angioplasty. Once the vessels have become occluded, bypass surgery is inevitable.

### *Femoro-femoral bypass graft*

Unilateral occlusion of an iliac artery, blocking the blood supply to one leg, can be treated by a femoro-femoral crossover graft (see Figure 6.6). This involves taking blood from the top of the good leg into the top of the affected leg. This procedure does not reduce the blood supply to the good leg, because the amount of blood flowing into the good leg is controlled by the run off. If the run off is improved by diverting some blood into the other leg, then the inflow also increases. This procedure can be carried out without opening the abdomen. It is very effective, relatively straightforward and certainly applicable to patients whose general condition is poor.

Figure 6.6   Femoro-femoral bypass

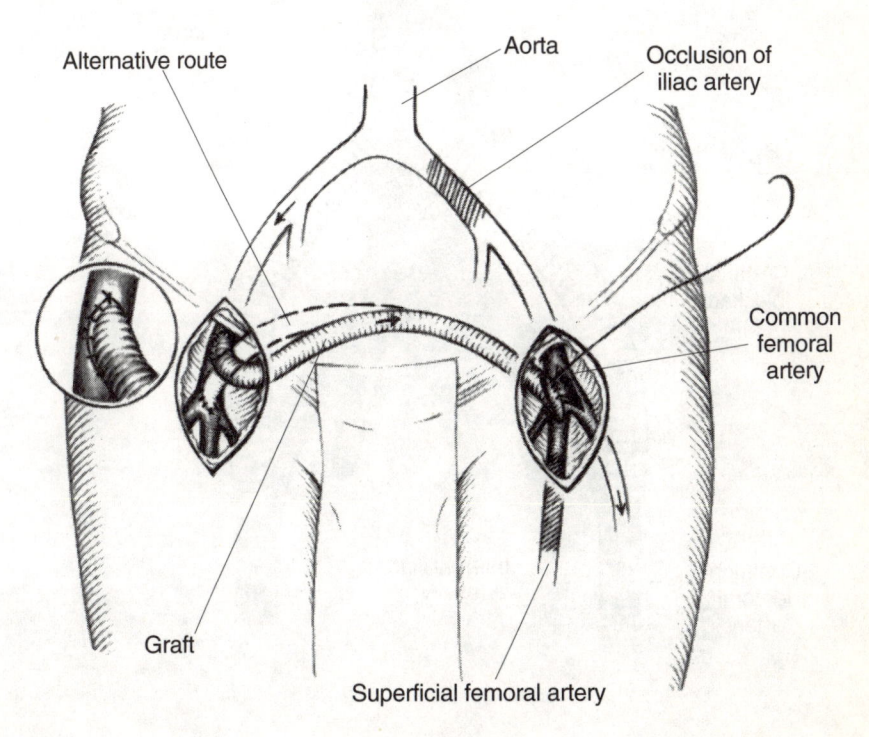

## Aorto-bifemoral bypass graft

If the aorta is severely diseased or occluded, or both iliac arteries are occluded, then a complete bypass taking blood from the aorta into the top of the legs can be carried out (an aorto bifemoral graft: see Figure 6.7). A synthetic trouser (shaped like a pair of trousers) graft is used. This is sewn directly into the aorta, then carried down into the top of the legs, where it is joined to the femoral arteries. Although this is a major procedure, the operation is extremely effective. The death rate of this procedure should be less than 1%, particularly when patients with serious heart problems have been excluded. The major complications that can arise include infection, blockage of the graft and blockage of small vessels supplying the bowel and the spinal cord. Blockage of the vessels supplying the bowel is usually recognised at the time of surgery and appropriate steps are taken. Blocking of the vessels supplying the spinal cord is unpredictable. Although this is an extremely rare complication, the results are devastating.

**Figure 6.7**     **Aorto bifemoral bypass**

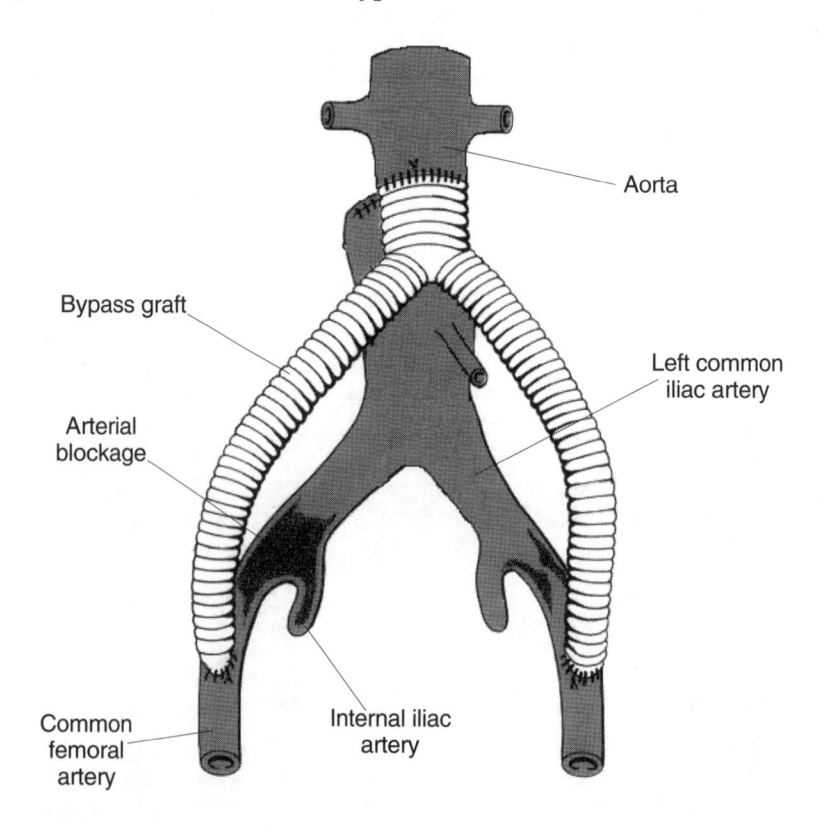

## Femoro-popliteal grafts

One of the most commonly affected arteries in arteriosclerosis is the superficial femoral artery. This is the main artery in the thigh, supplying blood to the leg below the knee. A femoro-popliteal bypass graft involves taking blood from the common femoral artery in the groin to the popliteal artery at the knee. Sometimes, this graft can be continued on below the knee and joined to vessels just above the ankle (femoro-distal bypass graft). The best graft involves using the patient's own long saphenous vein. Because the vein has valves in it, it is necessary to take the vein out, ligating all the branches, and turn it round, inserting the top end into the artery at the knee and the bottom end of the vein into the artery at the groin. An alternative procedure (in situ vein graft) involves separating the long saphenous vein in the groin and separating the long saphenous vein at the level of the knee. All branches are divided between the groin and the knee and then the vein is anastamosed to the artery. A special instrument is used to divide the valves so that blood can flow the wrong way through the vein.

Sometimes, the vein is unsuitable for bypass grafting and synthetic graft materials are used. These materials include PTFE (polytetralfluoroethylene) and woven dacron. The grafts are sutured into position at both the top and bottom end. Having completed the surgical procedure, it is important to check that there is good blood flow into the lower part of the leg. If there is any doubt about the success of this procedure, on-table arteriography or duplex ultrasound imaging can be carried out.

Before carrying out these surgical procedures, it is, again, important to make sure that the patient fully understands the nature of the operation and the potential complications. The purpose of the operation is to improve the blood supply to the lower leg and relieve symptoms such as rest pain or claudication. The main complication is failure. Even if the surgical procedure is carried out in the best units, a number of these grafts will fail. Failure of a graft may result in further surgery, which, in itself, may result in amputation. Another serious complication following arterial bypass grafts is infection. If the graft becomes infected, it may be necessary to remove it. This may involve further surgical procedures to restore the circulation to the lower leg or, sadly, may result in amputation.

# AMPUTATION

Amputation is generally carried out as a last resort. Before carrying out an amputation, the surgeon should ensure that there are no alternative procedures that can be carried out to save the circulation to the limb. An amputation can be carried out at any level and may involve the amputation of a single digit, of part of the foot, below the knee, above the knee or involve an amputation through a joint. The principal reason for performing an amputation is non-viable (dead) and infected tissue. Ischaemic pain (absent blood supply) is one of the most severe pains that you can experience. The pain itself is extremely debilitating and may lead to a very irrational patient. This, combined with age and infection, may make it extremely difficult for the patient to give consent. Following an amputation, the patient's well being improves dramatically and they may be able to return to an independent existence. Except in the emergency situation when there is overwhelming infection, patients should be formally assessed before undergoing an amputation. If the tissues in the leg are not dead, then vascular reconstruction may be practical.

Amputation is one of the oldest surgical procedures described. An amputation pre-anaesthesia used to take about three minutes. It is also an operation which, on one occasion, was associated with a 300% mortality. In carrying out an amputation of the leg, the 19th century surgeon, Linton, amputated the fingers on the hand of his assistant. As he swung round with the knife, the knife pierced the trousers of an observer, who died of fright. Linton's assistant, having had his fingers amputated, developed severe infection in the hand, spreading to the arm, which resulted in septicaemia (this was pre-antibiotics). The patient who had undergone the amputation also got infected and died. Even those surgeons providing lawyers with a regular source of income would have difficulty in achieving this today.

The level of amputation is really determined by the viability of the limb. There is nothing more depressing than to remove a toe today, a foot next week, the lower part of the leg the week after, finally finishing up with an above knee amputation. There are relatively few tests which will predict the success of an amputation. Attempts at measuring the blood flow in the skin have been carried out, but the majority of surgeons perform an amputation based on clinical assessment. The principle of an amputation is to cut through and reflect skin flaps. The muscle is then divided and reflected from the bone, and the bone is divided at a higher level. This allows the muscle to be sutured across the end of a bone and the skin flaps to be sutured across the end of a muscle. It is important that none of the tissues are under tension. Although the blood supply to the limb may be extremely poor, bleeding can occur and standard practice involves the use of drains to remove this blood. With high amputations, particularly when the blood supply is poor, prophylactic antibiotics are given to prevent clostridial infection (gas gangrene).

Following an amputation, a patient may be fitted with an artificial limb. Sadly, elderly patients are often confined to a wheelchair. The lower the amputation, the less disability the patient will suffer. Amputation of a digit requires no specified prosthesis. Amputation of part of the foot requires a modified shoe. A below knee amputation can be fitted with a boot. Above knee amputations require more complex prostheses which flex at the knee. Many of the old prostheses were supported by large belts and shoulder harnesses. The modern generation of prostheses are much lighter and are attached to the stump by a suction process.

Before carrying out an amputation, it is important to obtain the patient's consent. If the patient is toxic or confused, it may be necessary to obtain the consent from a relative. Before carrying out the procedure, the patient should, if possible, be told what the procedure involves and what an amputation will entail; the patient should also be given some idea as to how they can be rehabilitated, usually with an artificial limb. One of the major complications of which a patient should be aware is that, following an amputation, the stump may not heal. This may require a further surgical procedure.

Following the amputation of a limb, particularly for ischaemic pain, the patient may complain of phantom limb pain. The patient, even after amputation, feels that the limb is still present and the limb remains painful. This is an extremely irritating complication, and one which may prove difficult to treat. It is to prevent this complication that one encourages patients to undergo early amputation, if amputation is thought to be inevitable.

## THE DIABETIC FOOT

Although covered in part in other sections of this book, the diabetic foot deserves a special mention. Diabetes is extremely common, particularly with an ageing population. We recognise two forms of diabetes – the juvenile form of diabetes, which is usually insulin dependent, and maturity onset diabetes, which may be controlled by diet and oral hypoglycaemic agents. Both forms of diabetes are associated with arterial disease affecting both large and small vessels. In addition to the vascular problems, they also have a sensory neuropathy. This is an abnormality of the nerves, whereby the feet become less sensitive. As a result of decreased sensation in the feet, diabetic patients are more likely to injure themselves. The injury may simply be a blister occurring on the foot due to excessive walking, or may result from direct trauma, such as standing on a nail or a drawing pin. Diabetic patients may walk round for several days with a nail in the sole of their shoe without noticing an injury to their foot.

Because diabetic patients are more prone to infection, they have to be treated carefully.

When any patient presents with an ulcerated area on the foot or toes, diabetes should be excluded. These patients should then have a full history taken and undergo a proper examination, which includes palpation of the pulses. Pulses can be difficult to feel and, under these circumstances, a Doppler ultrasound stethoscope should be employed.

Most patients present to their general practitioner, who should have no hesitation in referring them for a surgical opinion.

## Vascular Surgery

If there are signs of arterial insufficiency and these signs include diminished pulses, pallor, pain (rest pain or claudication), signs of slow healing or evidence of uncontrolled infection, then a formal vascular assessment should be obtained. A vascular assessment will include measuring the ankle brachial pressure index, Duplex ultrasound scanning of the vessels and arteriography.

If there is evidence of large vessel disease, this can be treated with angioplasty or vascular reconstruction. Treatment with antibiotics and surgical debridement (which involves removing superficial dead tissue) should also be used.

Once the circulation to the limb has been restored or shown to be adequate, local debridement to control infection can be carried out. This may involve the removal of a digit, or a ray amputation (removal of a toe and part of the metatarsus: see Figure 6.8). Sometimes, partial amputation of the foot or a below knee or above knee amputation may be required.

**Figure 6.8    Ray amputation**

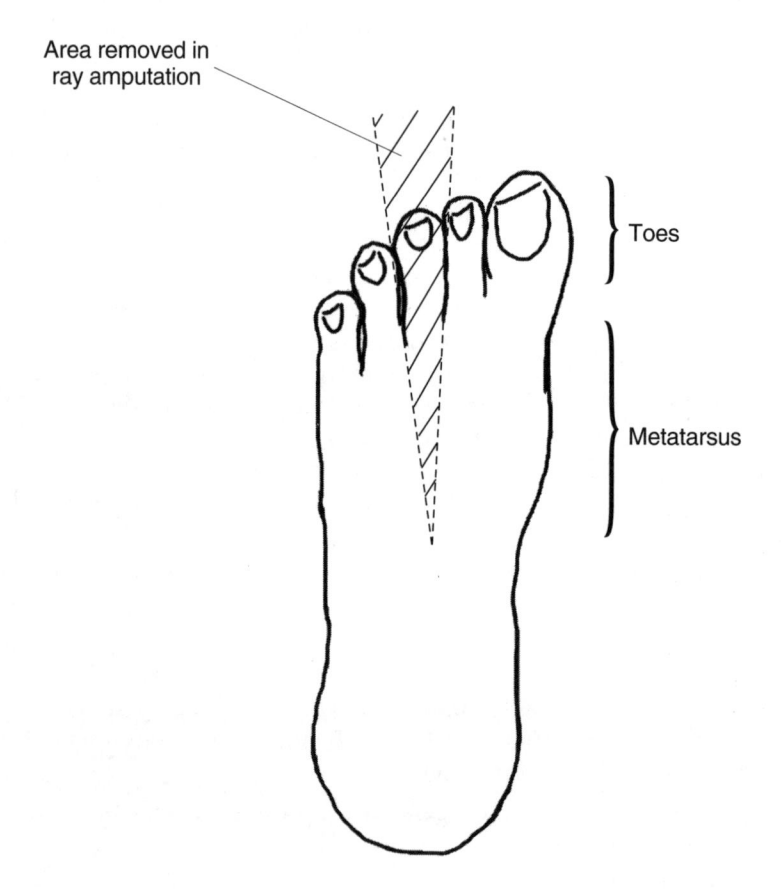

Because diabetic patients are prone to injury, great care should be given to their footwear. Careful chiropody and appropriate padding in the shoes should be used. Many diabetic foot problems arise simply due to shearing forces in the foot during walking, which result in tissue disruption beneath the surface followed by a cavity, infection and an ulcer.

There have been many medico-legal cases involving diabetic patients. Perhaps the single most common complaint is that the patient feels they have undergone an unnecessary amputation and that, with proper treatment, this could have been avoided. Unfortunately, amputation in diabetic patients is common and, in most cases, represents advancement of the disease and the difficulties involved in controlling the underlying medical condition and infection. There are, however, many diabetic patients who have good cause to complain. Amputation is not an inevitable outcome of diabetic foot ulceration.

In assessing a patient with view to preparing a medico-legal claim, the following factors may be helpful. It is important to establish when the problem arose and what, if any, treatment the patient has received. The patient may, in many instances, be unaware of when the problem arose. The examination forms the first part of any treatment regime and the thoroughness of this examination is important. If the doctor has failed to examine the limb and failed to note the presence of an underlying circulatory insufficiency, this may well represent unacceptable medical practice. Continuing treatment when the medical records clearly illustrate a deterioration is, again, unacceptable. A delay in referral, or a failure to appreciate the urgency of the situation may prejudice the outcome.

Some patients may be unsuitable for vascular reconstruction and amputation is inevitable. When there is evidence of infection, swabs need to be taken and appropriate antibiotics administered.

Unfortunately, these patients often have bilateral disease. It is extremely difficult to progress a case where a patient has lost a limb due to alleged negligence when their other limb is amputated six months later, despite proper care and attention. In these cases, liability may be accepted, but causation contested.

*Case*

### Diabetes, with arterial insufficiency

A 66 year old lady with a 15 year history of insulin dependent diabetes complained to her general practitioner of pain and discolouration in the big toe. The general practitioner diagnosed infection and treated her with antibiotics. No investigations were initiated. The general practitioner did not record whether pulses were present. Six weeks later, the patient had an ulcer on her toe and was referred to hospital for investigations. She was seen within three days and admitted the following day to undergo an urgent arteriogram. The arteriogram showed very extensive peripheral vascular disease with complete occlusion of the superficial femoral artery and a single vessel run off below the knee. A general practitioner report was obtained, which suggested that the patient should have been referred to hospital when first seen and should have undergone investigations. Liability was unlikely to be an issue. A vascular expert, on reviewing the X-rays, concluded that no attempt at reconstruction could have been carried out and that, although she could have been seen six weeks earlier, there was no specific treatment that could or should have been carried out.

*Case*

## Diabetes, with local injury and arterial insufficiency

A middle aged man with a 20 year history of insulin dependent diabetes presented to his general practitioner having trodden on a nail. The general practitioner observed the puncture site, made no examination of the patient but prescribed antibiotics and advised him to clean it. One week later, the patient returned to the general practitioner with a small discharging area on the sole of his foot. The general practitioner arranged for the district nurse to visit, to continue the dressings and continue antibiotics. Two weeks later (three weeks after the original injury), the patient complained of redness and swelling on the upper aspect of the foot. The general practitioner referred him to the local hospital, where he was examined and noted to have absent femoral, dorsalis pedis and posterior tibial pulses in that leg. His blood sugar was high and he had evidence of extensive infection within the foot. He received treatment for his diabetes and underwent arteriography. Arteriography revealed an iliac artery stenosis amenable to angioplasty (which was carried out) and evidence of arterial disease throughout the limb, with two vessel run off below the knee (three vessel run off is normal). Despite intravenous antibiotics, the infection spread and the patient underwent a below knee amputation. The patient's complaint was that, if the general practitioner had treated him properly in the first instance, he would not have undergone an amputation.

When the patient saw his general practitioner, the general practitioner did not examine the circulation. Had the general practitioner appreciated that the patient had a reduced circulation, and had he referred him to hospital, he would have undergone arteriography at that stage. A combination of restoring the circulation to the limb and effective antibiotics given by an intravenous route would probably have prevented the extensive infection in the foot and would probably have prevented the amputation. The general practitioner should have appreciated that diabetic patients do have arterial disease; he should also have appreciated the importance of early, aggressive treatment of foot lesions. Because diabetic patients have diminished sensation, the changes are often quite severe without the patient being aware.

Liability was not an issue, but the defendants argued that the patient would probably have lost his leg at some point. Diabetic patients are at risk of developing foot problems and local amputation of the toes or part of the foot is quite common. The patient lost his foot and lower leg partly because of the infection and partly because of unrecognised arterial disease, which, at that stage, was amenable to treatment. It is probable that this man's disease would have progressed and therefore, at some point, he would almost certainly have required either further surgery or amputation. An agreement was reached between both parties and the plaintiff received some compensation, but the compensation was reduced in view of the long term prognosis.

CHAPTER 7

# TREATMENT OF ARTERIAL DISEASE II

## ACUTELY ISCHAEMIC LIMB

A patient may present with a sudden onset of a painful, cold, pulseless limb. This represents a surgical emergency. The patient should be referred immediately to hospital, should undergo investigations and then undergo procedures to restore the circulation. When the blood supply to a limb becomes occluded suddenly, the patient will develop severe pain, initially in the foot, spreading back through the leg. They may complain that the foot is cold, it may feel numb, and it will certainly look pale. A comparison with the other leg may be made. Some patients may occlude the circulation to both limbs simultaneously (saddle embolus).

Sudden occlusion of the arterial supply to a limb can occur if foreign material, often thrombus originating in the heart, travels to the limb. The clot from the heart (embolus) becomes lodged when the vessel narrows or divides. Once the embolus is lodged, there is no further circulation beyond that. Sometimes, a complete occlusion can occur as the result of a local spontaneous thrombosis. This usually occurs in association with narrowing and pre-existing arteriosclerotic disease. If a patient presents to his general practitioner, the history, the appearance of the legs and the absence of pulses will allow the general practitioner to make the diagnosis of arterial insufficiency and refer the patient immediately to hospital. This represents a surgical emergency and delays in referral are quite unacceptable. When the patient is seen in hospital, a further examination will be carried out, followed by appropriate tests and treatment. If the problem has been caused by an embolus, it is likely that the patient will have evidence of heart disease. This may be apparent on the patient's history or evident from an electrocardiogram. In a patient with no past history of arteriosclerotic disease and evidence of cardiac disease, then a diagnosis of embolus may be made. If the patient has evidence of pre-existing peripheral vascular disease, then the differential diagnosis lies between an embolus and a thrombosis. Arteriography, either prior to conducting surgery or at the time of surgery, will reveal the true diagnosis.

### Embolectomy

An embolectomy is a simple surgical procedure which can be carried out in any surgical unit. The procedure can be carried out under general anaesthesia or under local anaesthesia. If the embolus is lodged in the leg, then, with appropriate anaesthesia, an incision is made to expose the femoral artery. Having exposed the femoral artery, clamps to control the flow of blood through the artery are placed across it. An incision is made in the artery and a fine catheter with a deflated balloon on the end of it (a Fogarty catheter) is passed up the artery to the aorta; the balloon is then inflated and the catheter is withdrawn. This should result in removal of any proximal clot and restoration of blood flow to the groin. The clamp is applied to control bleeding, the distal clamp is removed and the catheter is passed into the lower leg. It may be necessary to pass the catheter more than once, given that there are three separate vessels below the knee. Once all the clot has been removed from the artery and back bleeding established, the hole in the artery made for the insertion of the catheter can be closed. At the end of the surgical procedure, pulses should be present. If there is any doubt about the adequacy of the embolectomy, on-table arteriography can be carried out. The best results are achieved if embolectomy is carried out as soon as possible after the occlusion occurs.

**Acute thrombosis**

Where an acute thrombosis has occurred in an artery, it may be possible to remove it using an embolectomy (Fogarty) catheter. If there is evidence of severe peripheral vascular disease, arteriography followed by the infusion of a fibrinolytic agent, streptokinase or TPA (tissue plasminogen activator), may restore the circulation. Streptokinase or TPA may be used prior to surgery. If the circulation to the limb does not return, this approach is stopped and the patient undergoes surgery. Not all patients are suitable for surgery and this can only be determined following the arteriogram. The patient may need to undergo urgent arterial bypass surgery.

# SYMPATHECTOMY

Blood vessels are controlled by the autonomic nervous system. This is divided into the para-sympathetic and sympathetic systems. The autonomic nervous system functions without conscious control and is responsible for the maintenance of blood flow and temperature regulation, etc. The blood vessels have a good sympathetic supply, the sympathetic nerves causing them to constrict. Sympathectomy has, in the past, been widely performed for patients presenting with arterial disease. The place of sympathectomy is now reserved for a few clinical indications. In patients with skin ulceration due to arterial insufficiency, a sympathectomy may improve the circulation to the skin sufficiently to allow the ulcer to heal. A sympathectomy will not affect the large vessels, which, by this stage, are heavily calcified. There are a number of vaso-spastic conditions (for example, Raynaud's disease) which have, in the past, been treated by sympathectomy. Current treatment of Raynaud's disease involves medication, there being very few indications to carry out a sympathectomy.

The most common indication for carrying out a sympathectomy is for hyperhidrosis (excess sweating of the hands and armpits).

There are two approaches to sympathectomy: one chemical, the other surgical.

A chemical sympathectomy involves injecting an agent (phenol) in close proximity to the nerve to destroy it. A sympathectomy can be carried out in the cervical region or in the lumbar region. The purpose of both chemical and surgical sympathectomy is to damage a short segment of the sympathetic chain. A chemical sympathectomy is carried out under x-ray control, the tip of the needle being placed in close proximity to the sympathetic chain before an injection of Phenol is given.

## Cervical sympathectomy

A surgical sympathectomy involves removing a short segment of the chain, preserving the sympathetic supply to the head and neck. There are three approaches: (a) through the base of the neck; (b) an open approach through the axilla; and (c) a thoracoscopic approach, again through the axilla. Although there may be specific indications for each of these approaches, the thoracoscopic approach is now the most widely practised. The operation involves inserting a thoracoscope (very similar to the laparoscope), having partially deflated the lung by injecting carbon dioxide into the space between the lung and the rib cage. Under direct vision, the sympathetic chain can be visualised on the side of a vertebral body. A short segment of sympathetic chain from the base of the first rib to the third rib is removed. Any bleeding can be controlled by diathermy, but care must be taken not to use diathermy excessively at the lower border of the first rib. If the sympathetic chain is taken too high or excessive diathermy is used, the sympathetic supply to the head and neck can be disrupted. Disruption of the sympathetic supply to the head and neck results in Horner's syndrome, which consists of a droopy eyelid, a dilated pupil and dryness over the side of the face. It is the drooping eyelid and dilated pupil which are most obvious and which cause the patient to complain.

If the operation is being carried out for hyperhidrosis, the patient often notices an immediate effect. At some point during the first 24 hours there may be transient sweating but, once that has passed, the patient will have a dry hand and dry axilla.

Vascular Surgery

Before carrying out this operation, it is important that the patient appreciates the purpose of the procedure. Many patients undergoing a cervical sympathectomy for hyperhidrosis have a severe disability, being unable to write or type and regularly needing to dry their hands.

It is important that patients understand the operation and that there is a small but definite risk of developing Horner's syndrome.

Because the operation involves deflating the lung, most surgeons will only do one side at a time, the second side being carried out from one to three weeks later.

**Figure 7.1    Cervical sympathectomy**

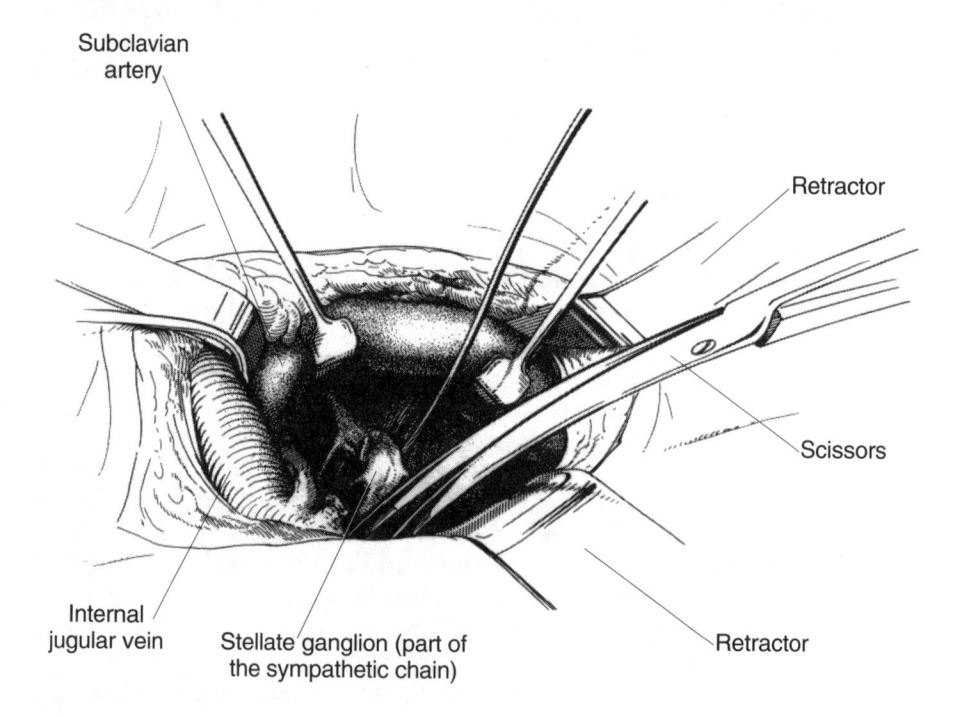

- Subclavian artery
- Retractor
- Scissors
- Internal jugular vein
- Stellate ganglion (part of the sympathetic chain)
- Retractor

*Case*

*Nerve injury following cervical sympathectomy*

A general practitioner referred a 60 year old woman with carpal tunnel syndrome, affecting both wrists, to a consultant surgeon.

She was seen by the consultant surgeon, who noted that the patient was complaining of paraesthesia in both hands but most of her troubles seemed to be due to quite marked colour changes in the fingers of both hands. She described her hands as going white and, occasionally, the tips going blue. She had marked pulp changes in the thumb of the right hand. The consultant surgeon thought her problem was due to Raynaud's phenomenon, and arranged for her to have a series of investigations. The consultant surgeon reviewed her. Immunological studies, rheumatoid factor and thyroid studies were all normal. An ESR (erythrocyte sedimentation rate) was 5 mm/hour (normal) and a full blood count differential was also normal. Urea and electrolytes and liver function tests were also normal. An X-ray of the cervical spine and thoracic inlet showed no cervical ribs, although there were minor spondylitic changes in the lower cervical spine. The consultant surgeon felt that her Raynaud's phenomenon would be best dealt with, initially, on medical lines and he started her on adalat 10 mg bd. He reviewed her again and recorded that her hands had improved considerably, probably due to the weather. She had developed a rash with the adalat, but was somewhat improved by praxilene. He suggested that she continued taking the praxilene and arranged to see her in November when the weather got colder. He felt it would be worth discussing bilateral sympathectomy with her then. He reviewed her, noting that the weather was colder and that her symptoms of Raynaud's were progressing. He made arrangements for her to come in for a bilateral cervical sympathectomy.

She was admitted to undergo surgery and a left cervical sympathectomy was performed. During the course of this operation, an injury occurred in the brachial plexus, to a major nerve supplying the left arm. In the immediate post-operative period, it became clear that she had weakness in the left arm. She was treated with physiotherapy but still has a residual problem.

There can be no justification for damaging major nerves. It is important to identify the nerves. Having damaged the nerve, this patient will be left with a considerable disability.

This relatively straightforward case is yet to settle. The defendants have argued that the nerve was within muscle and that, during the course of exposure, damage to the nerve was inevitable.

*Case*

*Axillary hyperhidrosis (sympathetic overactivity)*

Patients with excessive axillary sweating are often referred to vascular surgeons to undergo sympathectomy. Ms R presented with a long history of excessive sweating, affecting both the axillae and the hands.

She underwent bilateral cervical sympathectomies. The operation was carried out through the base of the neck.

Following the operation, the patient complained about the appearance of the scars and the fact that she was now sweating excessively elsewhere.

A cervical sympathectomy can be carried out through the base of the neck or through the axilla. In a young woman, a trans-axillary approach produces a better cosmetic result.

Although the surgeon cannot be criticised for using the neck approach, the patient should probably have been given more information, so that she could have made an informed decision as to which operation to undergo.

Excessive sweating from other areas of the body is a well recognised feature of this procedure and, again, the patient should have been warned in advance. There is nothing to suggest that there was any problem with the operation that has led to the excessive sweating.

After considerable discussions and medical reports, this case did not proceed.

## Lumbar sympathectomy

This operation involves making a small abdominal incision at the level of the umbilicus. The incision is placed laterally and the operation is carried out without entering the peritoneal cavity (retroperitoneal approach). By deepening the incision and moving the peritoneum forwards, access to the sympathetic chain from outside the peritoneal cavity can be achieved. The sympathetic chain is identified, running alongside the lumbar vertebrae, and a segment of chain from L2 to T12 is resected. Unlike cervical sympathectomy, both sides can be carried out at the same time. The operation on the right side is technically more difficult because of the presence of the inferior vena cava and large veins, which can bleed. Following the operation, the patient may develop quite extensive bruising and may develop a transient paralytic ileus, in which the gut stops functioning for 24 to 48 hours. Provided these problems are recognised and treated (by intravenous fluids), no long term consequences result.

# ARTERIO-VENOUS MALFORMATIONS

Arterio-venous malformations arise as a result of a developmental abnormality. In their simplest form, they may present as birth marks. More complex arterio-venous malformations may result in considerable swelling, deformity, and abnormality in limb growth. They can occur on the skin, in the limbs or in organs, including the brain, liver and kidney. Some arterio-venous malformations present at birth simply thrombose and disappear. Others may continue to increase in size, requiring further investigations and treatment. Any patient presenting with a significant arterio-venous malformation should undergo duplex ultrasound imaging and arteriography. These investigations assess the extent of the lesion and a multidisciplinary approach to the treatment is then usually undertaken. Some arterio-venous malformations can be treated by embolisation. This involves inserting an arterial catheter into the vessel feeding the malformation, and then embolising the malformation with foam or cyanoacrylate (superglue). Sometimes, direct surgical incision followed by plastic surgical reconstruction may be necessary. In extreme situations, amputation of a limb may also be carried out.

## VOLKMANN'S ISCHAEMIC CONTRACTURE

If the blood supply to a limb is interrupted, then the oxygen already in the limb rapidly becomes used up. The limb can survive for a period of time without irreversible damage. If a tourniquet is applied to the limb, it is safe to do this for a period of time not exceeding two hours, during which time the limb survives without using oxygen. This results in a build-up of lactic acid in the limb and local damage to the capillaries occurs. When the tourniquet is released, there is an inflow of blood, with the limb going bright red (a hyperaemic response). Some leakiness at the capillaries occurs and this is known as a re-perfusion injury. There may be some swelling in the tissues, but this settles rapidly.

If the blood supply is cut off for longer, the tissues become irreversibly damaged. Some tissues can survive longer than others. The muscles are quite sensitive and, after two hours, will start to die. As the muscles die, they become replaced with fibrous tissue and this results in a contracture (Volkmann's ischaemic contracture).

Where a limb has had the blood supply interrupted for quite a long period of time and the blood supply is then restored, there is a risk of this contracture developing. The presence of this contracture therefore indicates the blood supply to the limb has been cut off for quite a long period of time. In severe cases, the entire muscle can die and may need surgical excision. With very severe cases the whole limb may die, resulting in gangrene and amputation.

*Case*

*Volkmann's ischaemic contracture*

Mrs M presented to her general practitioner, complaining about the fingers of her right hand being numb and pale. The general practitioner diagnosed Raynaud's disease and advised her to wear a glove and keep the arm warm.

The following day, she consulted him again with the same symptoms and was given the same advice.

The general practitioner did not examine the arm and did not check the radial pulse.

## Vascular Surgery

On the third day, she again complained of pain in the arm. On this occasion, she was seen by a different general practitioner, who noticed the absence of a radial pulse. A vascular opinion was sought and she was noted to have no brachial and no radial pulse. A cardiological examination revealed her to have an atrial fibrillation (an irregular heart beat). A probable diagnosis of brachial artery embolus was made and this was confirmed by arteriography. She underwent exploration of the brachial artery, with removal of an embolus. The circulation to the fingers was restored but, unfortunately, the circulation to the muscles in the forearm was irreversibly compromised. This resulted in loss of muscle and a fibrous contracture.

Liability was admitted and this case settled.

### Case

### *Development of a compartment syndrome while using a tourniquet*

A 33 year old man, with a history of diaphysial aclasis and multiple previous operations for removal of exostoses (bony lumps), was admitted for removal of yet another exostosis from the proximal part of his right tibia. The operation was apparently done under tourniquet control. The tourniquet was inflated for one hour and 20 minutes.

Following his return to the ward, he lost blood from the wound and had to be returned to theatre, where it was discovered that his anterior tibial artery and vein had been lacerated. The resultant haematoma was evacuated and the vessels were ligated. He subsequently developed a compartment syndrome and required resection of dead muscle. He needed split skin grafting and numerous examinations under anaesthetic.

On leaving hospital, he had very limited function of his right leg and was unable to dorsiflex his ankle. He also had a neurological deficit, requiring a permanent brace on his right leg.

The patient underwent a relatively straightforward operation, during the course of which, damage occurred to the tibial artery and veins. This resulted in a haematoma which resulted in pressure, leading to a compartment syndrome and the loss of some muscle and skin.

Damage to the anterior tibial artery and vein would not normally result in such extensive changes. The defence argued that to make the diagnosis and to institute treatment which would have altered the outcome, it would have been necessary to perform an arteriogram. Had an arteriogram been performed, injuries to the tibial artery would have been noted. It is probable that treatment would have involved ligation of the anterior tibial artery and that this, therefore, would not have affected the outcome. Because of the close proximity to the tibial artery, damage is a well recognised complication. Simply damaging the artery could therefore not be considered indicative of substandard medical treatment. Having damaged the artery, reconstruction was unlikely to be effective and, therefore, the outcome was inevitable.

Following a conference and lengthy discussions, including the advice of two other vascular surgeons, it was felt this case could not proceed.

*Case*

### Compartment syndrome, secondary to compression

Mr H was involved in a road traffic accident and sustained an injury to his right leg. He was taken to hospital and noted to have a fractured fibula. The leg was treated by immobilisation in a plaster cast. Mr H complained of pain and was treated with analgesics. He was seen on four separate occasions by his general practitioner and, on two occasions, in the hospital. After a period of 10 days, his toes were noted to look pale and the plaster cast removed. The circulation to the foot looked poor and an examination with a Doppler probe revealed the absence of either foot pulse. A diagnosis of compartment syndrome, secondary to compression, was made and he underwent fasciotomies. This is a procedure to relieve the pressure in the fascial compartments in the legs. Despite undergoing a fasciotomy, he lost a considerable amount of muscle in the leg which has left him with an ankle deformity and loss of muscle bulk.

This was a relatively minor injury associated with considerable swelling. The plaster cast was too tight and this resulted in an obstruction to the circulation and subsequent muscle damage. This was an avoidable complication and should not have occurred.

## SURGICAL COMPLICATIONS

Complications can occur following any surgical procedure. The complications may be early, occurring at the time of, or immediately after, the surgery, or late, occurring more than 24 hours after the completion of the surgical procedure. The complications may be specifically related to the surgical procedure or there may be complications related to surgery in general, that is, anaesthesia, breathing complications, renal or cardiac problems. It is impossible to avoid all complications but, with good pre-operative preparation and careful surgical technique, complications can be minimised. Some complications commonly occur with some procedures and, if this is the case, the patient should be advised of this before carrying out the procedure. Some complications are extremely rare but, even with good surgical technique, may occur. Complications which are likely to have a major effect on the patient's life following the procedure should be explained in full.

In an attempt to minimise complications, patients are assessed pre-operatively for their fitness to undergo surgery, to make sure that they have no pre-existing medical conditions which might be exacerbated by the surgery, and to give them prophylaxis, if appropriate, to stop them developing specific complications (deep vein thrombosis, infection).

Some complications, that is, bleeding and infection, may accompany any surgical procedure. Minor to moderate bleeding and minor infections seldom cause any long term problems. Specific complications are dealt with under each operation. Infection is a common complication of any surgical procedure. The majority of infections occur as a result of the patient's own skin organisms entering the wound at the time of surgery. Prior to carrying out surgery, the skin is cleaned, but this does not always prevent infection. The presence of a haematoma (a collection of blood) also increases the risk of local infection. When inserting prosthetic graft material, an infection represents a serious complication and may lead to the removal of the graft and even the loss of a limb. In an attempt to reduce the risk of infection, most patients undergoing a prosthetic implant will receive prophylactic antibiotics.

When a patient shows signs of infection, it is important to take bacteriological swabs and start the patient on appropriate antibiotics. Once an infection becomes deep seated, it may be necessary to remove all foreign material, including sutures and grafts.

## FUTURE DEVELOPMENT

Vascular surgery is a rapidly changing speciality. Most of the developments within vascular surgery have taken place within the last 50 years, with the majority of developments taking place within the last 10 years. There has been a total revolution in imaging services. Primary assessment is now carried out, in many centres, non-invasively. The diagnosis of arterial insufficiency can be carried out by duplex ultrasound imaging. Digital subtraction angiography is replacing routine standard angiography and magnetic resonance imaging is providing a facility to image the vessel in patients where contrast materials may be contraindicated (for example, renal patients). Advances in imaging techniques and the use of three-dimensional images will become standard practice.

Angioplasty and stenting procedures have reduced the number of open surgical procedures by 50%. Techniques are being developed to cross total occlusions, and to dilate these arteries, avoiding the need for open surgery.

Keyhole surgery for vascular patients is also being developed. Although there are limitations to the procedures currently being carried out, arteries can be replaced, bypassed or opened up using percutaneous techniques. Aneurysms can be treated by inserting a new liner percutaneously. These procedures, collectively referred to as endoluminal procedures, are currently being developed and evaluated.

Vascular surgery, like many other aspects of medicine, is a rapidly changing area. New procedures for previously untreatable conditions are being developed and better procedures for existing problems are being introduced.

New procedures may have an uncertain outcome and may be associated with unrecognised complications. Despite this, it is reasonable to evaluate these procedures, to refine them and to introduce them into general clinical practice.

# CHAPTER 8

# INVESTIGATION OF VENOUS DISEASE

## INTRODUCTION

Varicose veins remain one of the most common medical conditions presenting to doctors. They are also the commonest form of venous disease. The majority of patients with varicose veins will be managed by taking a history, a simple clinical examination and then appropriate treatment.

Not all cases of patients with venous disease, including patients with varicose veins, are straightforward. Some patients will already have received treatment, while others will be presenting with complications arising from their venous disease. Whilst it would be wrong to suggest that all patients with venous disease should undergo the following investigations, the principles of managing patients remain the same, no matter how simple or straightforward the underlying disease is.

## HISTORY

Any patient presenting with vein or vein-related problems should have a full history taken. The history should include current symptoms, duration of symptoms and whether the patient has undergone any previous treatment. It is important to determine whether there is a past history of any other medical problems and, in particular, surgical procedures. Specific inquiries should be made as to whether the patient has suffered any injuries to the leg (could they have a previous deep vein thrombosis?). In women, it is necessary to establish whether they are taking any hormones, either for contraception or hormone replacement therapy.

## EXAMINATION

Whilst venous disease can affect the upper limbs, 95% of patients present with venous disease affecting the lower limbs. It is important to undress the patient, to have them standing and to have them in a room with good lighting. Superficial veins tend to disappear when the patient lies flat.

## Inspection

The leg should be inspected, and the following things noted:

(a) the presence of veins;
(b) the position of these veins in relation to the front or the back of the leg;
(c) the presence or absence of colour changes;
(d) the presence or absence of skin changes around the lower part of the leg;
(e) any previous scars; and
(f) whether there is any apparent deformity of one or other leg.

## Palpation

With the patient standing, the groin should be palpated for the presence of a lump (a sapheno varix); the veins can then be palpated along their length. Communicating veins between the deep and the superficial system may be palpated, although this is not particularly reliable.

## Auscultation

The blood in the veins is relatively static and it is unusual to hear any sounds. If a patient has narrowing of the main veins at the top of the leg, a venous hum may be audible. Unlike the arterial system with turbulence, a venous hum is a much more prolonged and consistent sound.

# DOPPLER/ULTRASOUND STETHOSCOPE

Listening with a Doppler stethoscope over a normal vein achieves nothing. By compressing the calf or by getting the patient to take deep breaths in and out, augmented venous flow occurs, which can be detected with a Doppler ultrasound stethoscope. Whilst this will indicate the presence of flow, it does not exclude partial occlusion. The absence of venous flow may indicate total obstruction (a possible deep vein thrombosis); the presence of some flow, however, does not exclude a partially occluding thrombus. A bi-directional Doppler stethoscope would indicate the direction of flow and, in particular, indicate the presence of reflux. Reflux occurs when the blood flows the wrong way through the superficial veins. Venous blood should flow up the leg and from superficial to deep. Blood flowing from deep to superficial or flowing down the leg indicates reflux, and this is abnormal.

Investigation of Venous Disease

## PHOTOPLETHYSMOGRAPHY

Photoplethysmography measures small changes in the volume of blood beneath the skin surface. The technique involves shining light into the skin. This light is reflected depending on the amount of blood present in the vessels immediately deep to the skin surface. The probe is placed on the lower part of the leg just above the medial malleolus and the patient is asked to flex the ankle 10 times. Blood will be pumped out of the surface vessels, resulting in a measurable change in light reflection. When the patient stops moving the ankle, there is a slow refilling. The normal refilling is in excess of 15 seconds. If a patient has varicose veins, the refilling can occur not only by the arterial system (normal), but also by reflux through the veins (abnormal). This test provides a useful quick screening method for varicose veins and simple venous disease. The application of rubber bands above or below the knee in the presence of varicose veins and superficial vein reflux will correct these abnormalities, in the absence of deep vein problems.

**Figure 8.1** **Photoplethysmography**

## STRAIN GAUGE PLETHYSMOGRAPHY

This involves placing a circular band around the leg which responds to changes in volume. As the leg swells, the band is stretched and its conductivity altered. In a normal limb, the application of a tourniquet around the upper thigh will result in leg swelling. This swelling is detected by the strain gauge around the lower part of the leg. There is a slow but progressive change which corresponds to the swelling of the leg. When the tourniquet is released, blood flows from the leg rapidly. This rapid flow of blood from the leg results in a rapid return to the previous conductivity. If the venous outflow is obstructed, for example, with a deep vein thrombosis, then there will be a very slow return to the normal conductivity, indicating the presence of venous obstruction.

# Investigation of Venous Disease

**Figure 8.2** **Strain gauge plethysmography**

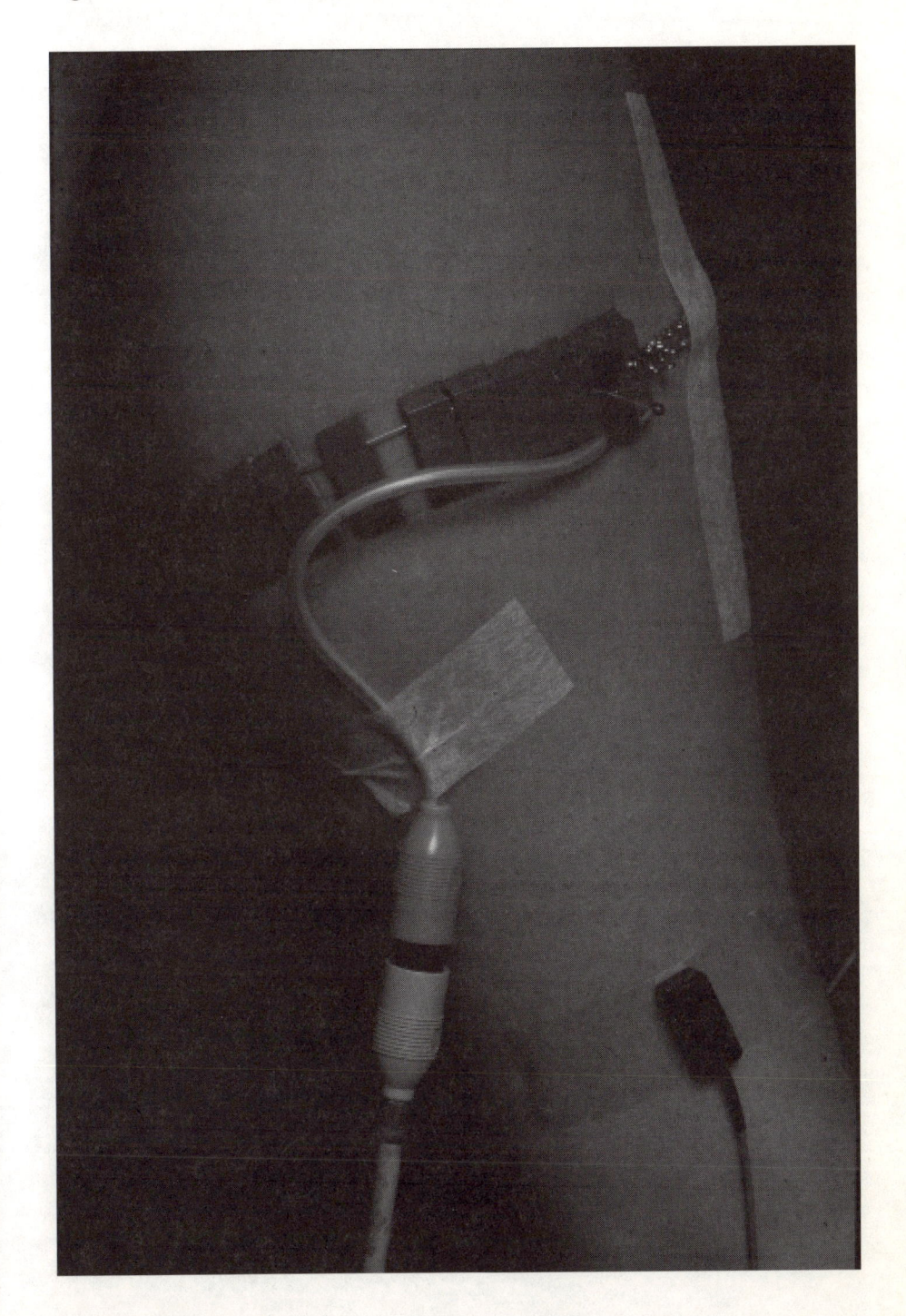

## DUPLEX ULTRASOUND IMAGING

Duplex ultrasound imaging (see Figures 8.3–8.5; see, also, Figure 5.2) has now become the principal tool for investigating patients with venous disease. The principle of duplex ultrasound imaging has been described (see Chapter 5). It is now widely used in the diagnosis of deep vein thrombosis, in the diagnosis of deep or superficial venous insufficiency and in the management of patients with venous ulcers. It provides both anatomical and physiological information about the venous system. Although it is becoming widely available, it may still not be present in all hospitals. It is dependent on having a good vascular technologist or a radiologist experienced in its use.

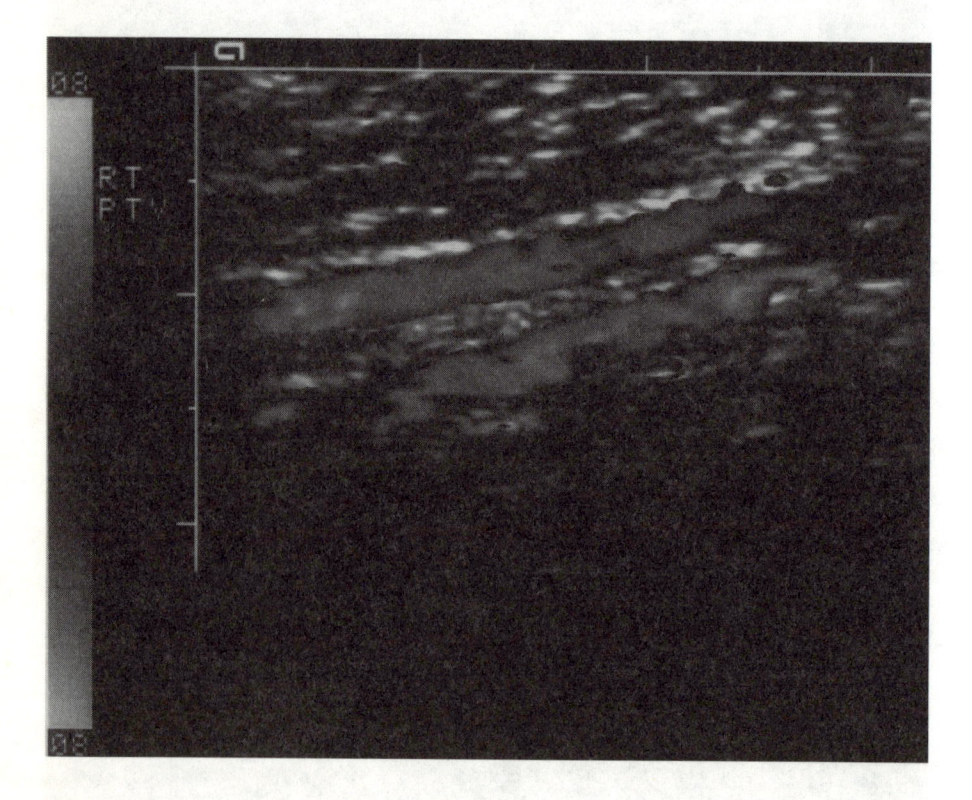

Figure 8.3    Duplex ultrasound image of posterior tibial veins in the calf

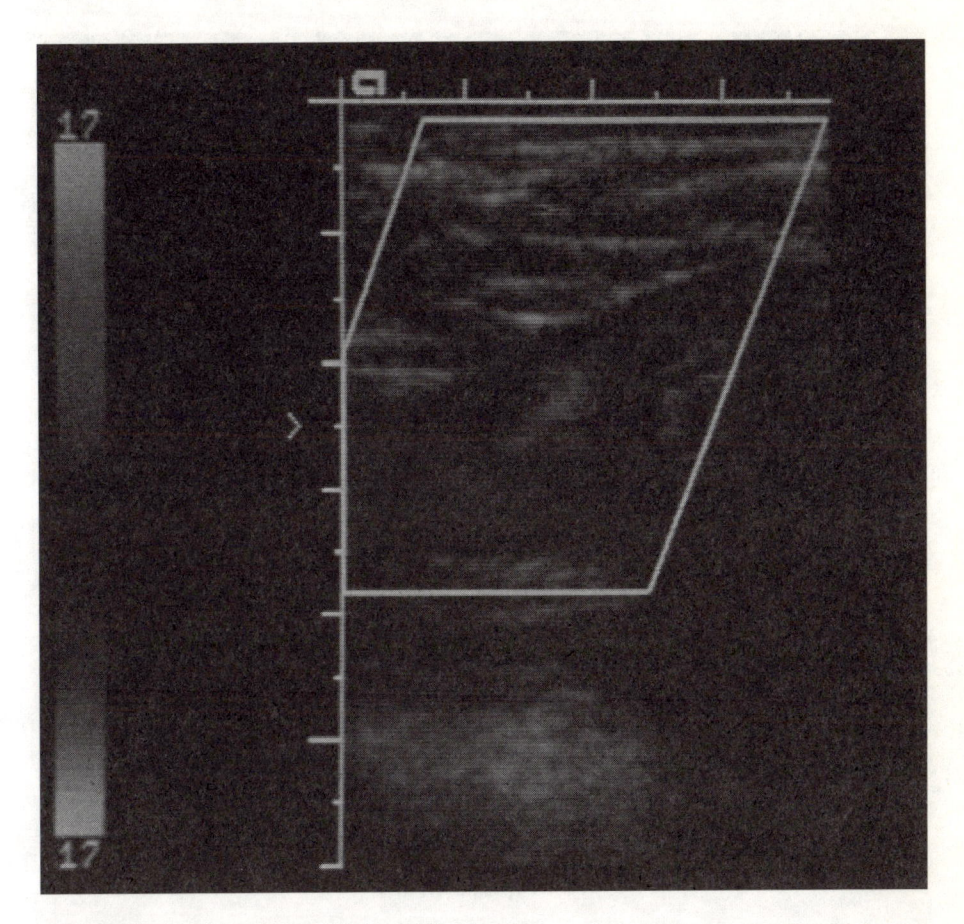

**Figure 8.4**     Duplex ultrasound image of the sapheno-femoral junction

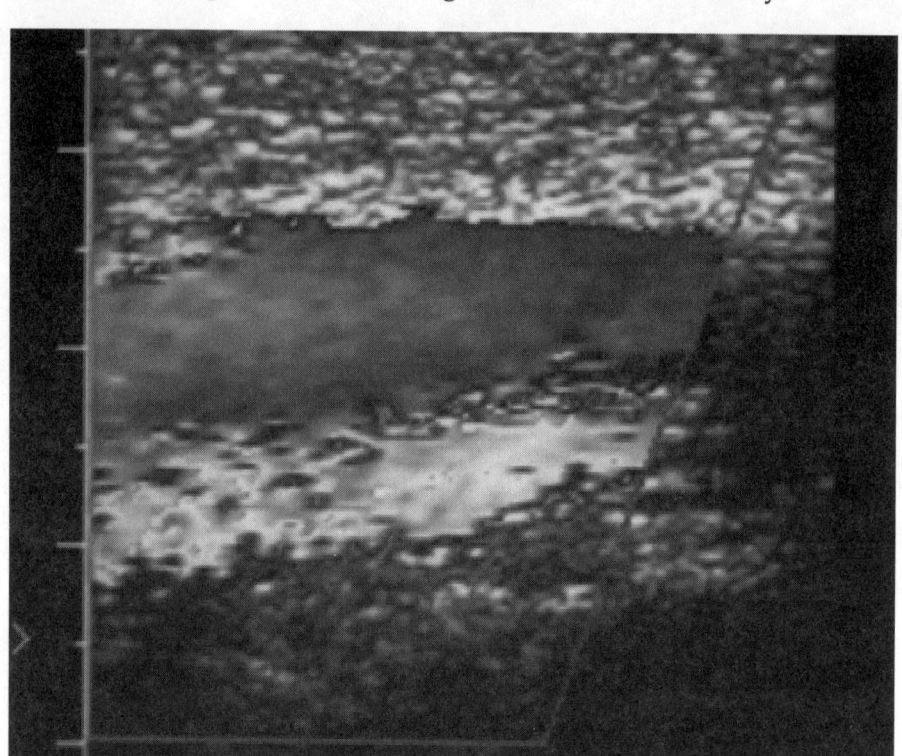

**Figure 8.5**  Duplex ultrasound image of femoral vein and artery

# VENOGRAPHY

Venography (see Figure 8.6) was the investigation by which all others were compared in the management of venous disease. It is now being replaced by duplex ultrasound imaging in many centres. Venography involves the injection of radio-opaque dye into superficial veins at the foot. A tourniquet around the ankle forces the contrast material into the deep veins and X-rays of the deep veins can then be taken. Venography is a relatively straightforward procedure and can be carried out in any hospital X-ray department with relatively straightforward equipment. It is not difficult to obtain good views of the calf and thigh veins, though it is sometimes very difficult to obtain good views of the ileofemoral segments (veins in the lower part of the abdomen). The X-rays will demonstrate the presence of veins, the patency of veins, and the presence or absence of filling defects (thromboses). Valves may also be visualised on the venogram, although special techniques are required to do this.

**Figure 8.6** **Venogram, showing right common femoral vein with a narrowed segment**

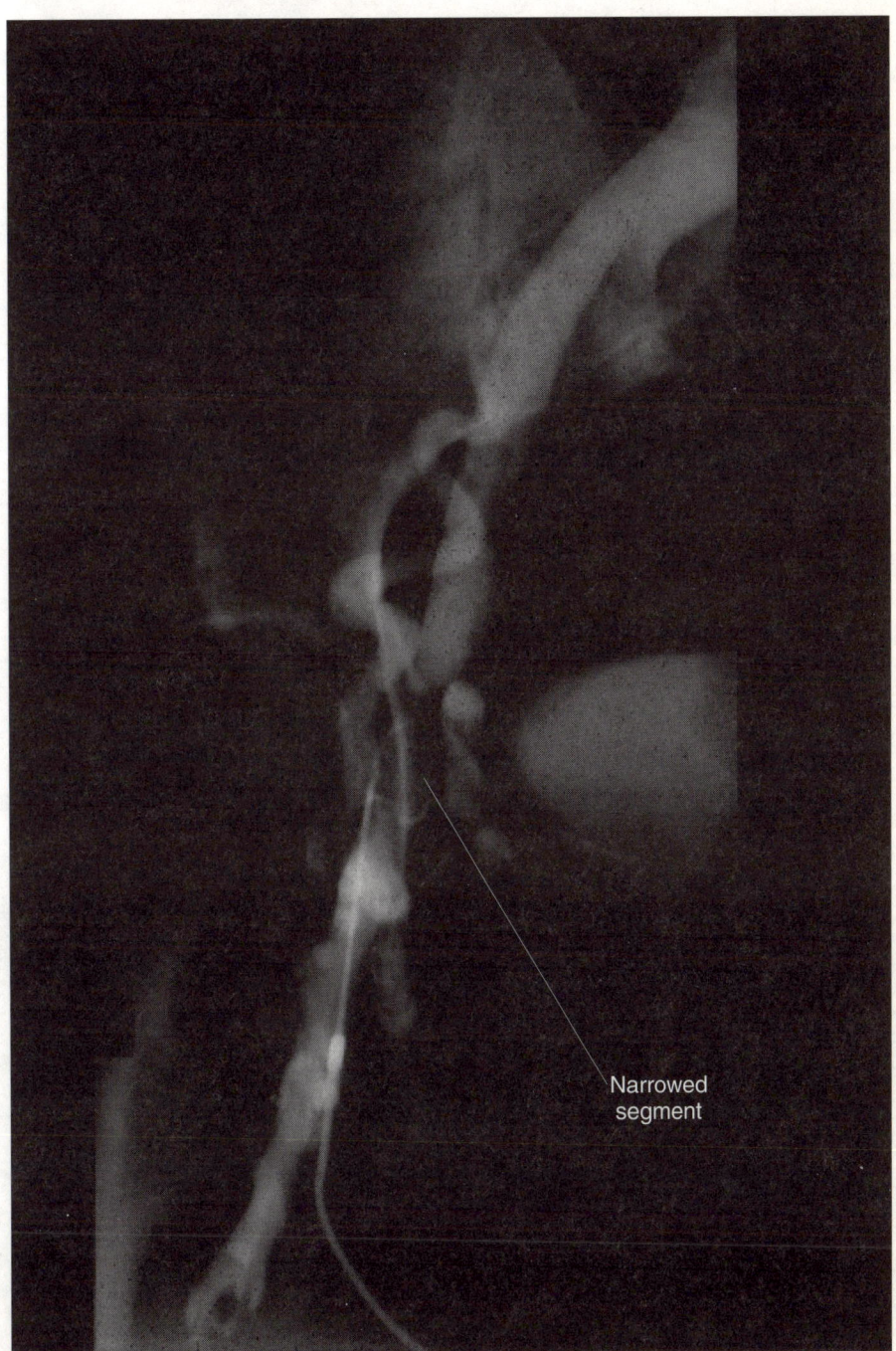

# CHAPTER 9

# TREATMENT OF VENOUS DISEASE

## DEEP VEIN THROMBOSIS

The blood in the arteries and veins remains liquid because of a fine balance between factors trying to make it clot and stop bleeding, and factors acting to prevent the blood setting. Factors which cause the blood to clot are thrombogenic, and those factors which keep the blood liquid are thrombophyllic. Just as some patients have a tendency to bleed (haemophiliacs), some patients also have a tendency to clot. A clot can occur in any vessel – arteries or veins. Clots in superficial veins seldom give rise to serious problems, although they can be associated with considerable pain. If blood sets in the deep veins – and these are the central veins, called deep veins because they run beneath an encircling layer of fibrous tissue (deep fascia) – then it may block the outflow of blood from the limb. Ninety five per cent of deep vein thromboses occur in the lower limb and pelvic vessels. An obstruction to the deep veins can cause swelling, pain, discomfort and dilatation of the superficial veins (see Figure 9.1). These signs and symptoms may or may not be present. It is possible to have very extensive deep vein thrombosis with no apparent signs or symptoms. Over half the patients who have a deep vein thrombosis have no signs or symptoms and, sometimes, to cause further difficulty, the signs which we would attribute to deep vein thrombosis may be caused by other factors. A rupture of a calf muscle, a rupture of a cyst behind the knee and minor trauma can all cause the leg to swell with redness and pain. The clinical diagnosis of a deep vein thrombosis may be extremely difficult and, for that reason, tests are relied upon in order to make the diagnosis.

**Figure 9.1** **Deep vein thrombosis**

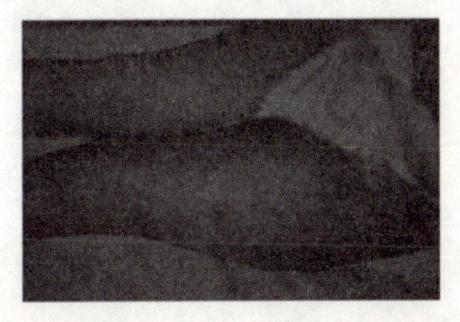

Swollen leg due to obstruction of the main vein

Deep vein thrombosis is important because it is associated with two important complications. The first complication occurs soon after the development of a deep vein thrombosis, when a segment breaks off and travels to the lung. If it is a small clot, the patient may not even feel this. If it is a large clot, it may result in instantaneous death. If the clot does not break off, it becomes organised and slowly, over a period of many months, may dissolve. Although the clot can be removed by the body's own natural defence system (the fibrinolytic system), valves in the deep veins may remain permanently damaged.

It is damage to the valves in the deep veins which leads to the post-thrombotic syndrome. This develops 10–15 years after an acute deep vein thrombosis and is characterised by pain, swelling, skin discolouration and ulceration. The condition does not always follow a deep vein thrombosis and its development depends on the extent of damage to the deep veins and, in particular, to the valves.

## Diagnosis of deep vein thrombosis

The clinical signs and symptoms of deep vein thrombosis are very unreliable. If a clinician suspects a diagnosis of deep vein thrombosis, whether there be clinical signs or not, then further investigation should be carried out. There are two investigations now used in routine clinical practice. One is venography (see Figure 9.2), which can be performed in all hospitals. It involves the injection of contrast material into the superficial veins in the foot. A tourniquet applied around the ankle forces the contrast material into the deep veins. X-rays taken will then reveal evidence of clot in the deep veins. This procedure, although widely available, is invasive and can be associated with quite significant discomfort. Duplex ultrasound imaging is also now widely used in the diagnosis of deep vein thrombosis. Duplex ultrasound imaging is non-invasive, and the investigation can be repeated. However, this investigation relies on an experienced technician to perform it. It gives information about the presence or absence of the deep vein thrombosis and information about the extent and age of the clot.

**Figure 9.2    Venogram, showing deep vein thrombosis**

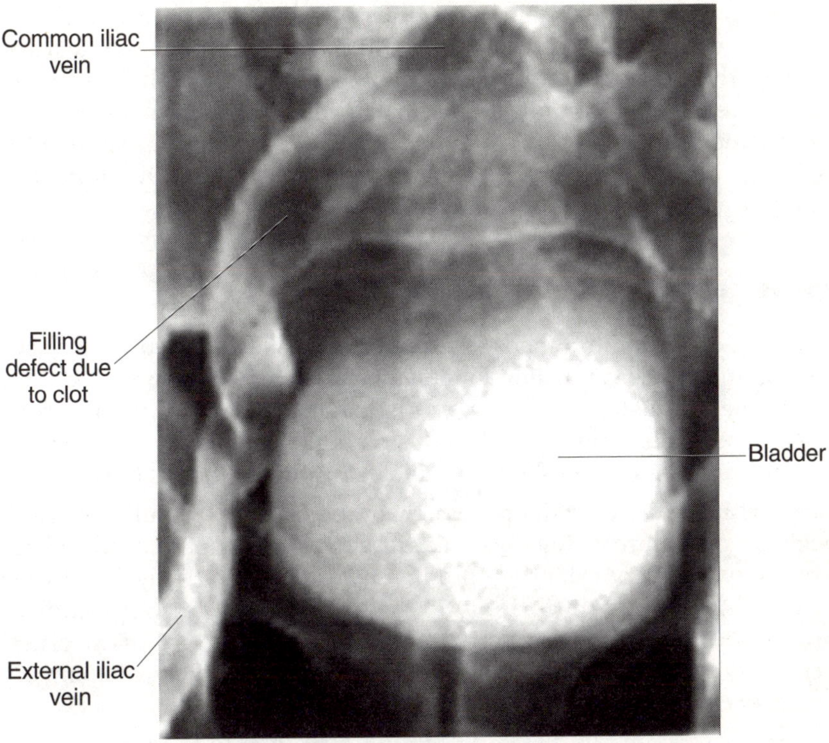

Common iliac vein

Filling defect due to clot

Bladder

External iliac vein

## Treatment of deep vein thrombosis

The standard treatment of a patient presenting with a deep vein thrombosis is to anticoagulate them. Heparin is a very effective anticoagulant and works almost immediately. The disadvantage of heparin is that it has to be given either by an intravenous injection or, more recently, by subcutaneous injection. Although it is possible to treat patients on an out-patient basis with subcutaneous heparin, the majority of patients are still admitted to hospital and receive a full course of intravenous heparin. Anticoagulation using tablets takes three to five days to become effective. It is now standard practice to administer an oral anticoagulant on admission to hospital. The dose of oral anticoagulant is adjusted using simple blood tests to measure clotting. The INR (international normalised ratio) expresses a ratio of the patient's clotting ability to normal. In the treatment of deep vein thrombosis, the aim is to achieve an INR of 2.5 to 3.5. Once the INR has reached 2.5, heparin can be stopped. When treating patients with anticoagulants there is a risk of bleeding. If too much anticoagulant is given, and that includes both heparin and oral anticoagulant, then the patient is at risk of bleeding. The dose of both Heparin and oral anticoagulants can be adjusted to maintain an effective level of anticoagulation without causing serious bleeding complications. Some patients are difficult to control and require very frequent blood tests. Sometimes, the concurrent administration of antibiotics, aspirin or excess alcohol intake can also complicate the management of these patients. Oral anticoagulants will usually be continued for between four and six months before being stopped. If the patient has had a previous deep vein thrombosis, there may be a case for continuing oral anticoagulation for life.

## Extensive deep vein thrombosis

Sometimes, a deep vein thrombosis is very extensive. If the deep veins in the limb are occluded, the circulation to the limb can become compromised. This is an extremely unusual condition and is usually associated with serious underlying medical problems. Total occlusion of the venous outflow is one of the few indications for surgical intervention in an attempt to save the limb.

Surgical removal of a deep vein thrombosis is extremely unusual, although the procedure is described and does have a few specific indications. Sometimes, with a very extensive thrombosis, drugs which actively dissolve clot are given. These are fibrinolytic drugs and include streptokinase, urokinase and plasminogen activators. These drugs are, themselves, associated with complications and cannot be given immediately after surgery because they cause excessive bleeding.

If there is a risk of clot breaking off and travelling to the lungs, or if a patient has already had a pulmonary embolism and shown signs of further emboli, despite anticoagulation, then the insertion of an inferior vena cava filter may be appropriate. An inferior vena cava filter is inserted into the inferior vena cava, the main vein running from the lower abdomen to the heart. These devices are now inserted using a simple percutaneous technique carried out under x-ray control. Once inserted, these devices usually remain permanently.

## Prevention of deep vein thrombosis

Deep vein thrombosis is associated with two major complications, pulmonary embolism and the development of a post-thrombotic limb. It follows, therefore, that if deep vein thrombosis can be prevented, both these complications can be avoided.

In 1856, Virchow, a German surgeon, described a triad of conditions which predispose to the development of a deep vein thrombosis. He described venous stasis, damage to the vein walls and an alteration in the coagulability of the blood predisposing to clotting. We now know that one or all of these factors may occur during hospital admissions and during surgical procedures. Spontaneous deep vein thrombosis is extremely rare but, in 1972, it was clearly demonstrated that a third of patients being admitted to hospital over the age of 40 years to undergo major surgical procedures would develop a deep vein thrombosis. Major orthopaedic procedures, particularly orthopaedic procedures associated with fractures of the hip in elderly patients, are associated with an even greater incidence of deep vein thrombosis. It is not only surgical patients who are at risk of developing a deep vein thrombosis but also medical patients, including those patients who have had myocardial infarction and stroke. Another important group of patients who may be at risk of developing a deep vein thrombosis are airline passengers who take long flights, during which time they remain totally immobile and suffer fluid depletion.

There have been many studies in surgical patients demonstrating the potential benefit of prophylactic measures to prevent deep vein thrombosis. The prophylactic measures available to patients undergoing surgical treatment in hospital include both mechanical methods and pharmacological methods. The mechanical methods include graduated compression stockings, intermittent pneumatic compression devices which sequentially squeeze the calf, and mechanical devices which flex or compress the foot. Pharmacological methods of preventing deep vein thrombosis include low doses of heparin, which can be administered subcutaneously, low doses of oral anticoagulants and a number of drugs, which include anti-platelet agents. More recently, highly refined forms of heparin (low molecular weight heparin) have been developed, which appear safer, have a lower incidence of bleeding complications and are equally or even more effective in the prevention of deep vein thrombosis and pulmonary embolism.

Despite clear evidence that the use of low dose heparin and various mechanical methods of prevention of deep vein thrombosis are effective, there has been a general reluctance to accept this into clinical practice. The main reason given for not using deep vein thrombosis prophylaxis is that these methods may be associated with increased bleeding complications and increased bleeding complications may be associated with an increased risk of infection. There is very little evidence to support this but, unfortunately, there is still a large and reputable body of medical opinion who do not recommend the use of DVT prophylaxis. Whilst it might be argued that a decision not to use DVT prophylaxis represents clinical judgment, this is contrary to the scientific evidence.

Where a surgeon fails to use DVT prophylaxis, he needs to have enhanced surveillance and may need to perform investigations to exclude a deep vein thrombosis in the immediate post-operative period.

Any patient being admitted to hospital who receives no deep vein thrombosis assessment and/or prophylaxis, and who then goes on to develop a deep vein thrombosis and pulmonary embolism, has grounds to complain. By way of a defence, the surgeon may argue that, by giving deep vein thrombosis prophylaxis, he would compromise the operation by increasing the risk of bleeding, which could result in infection. He may also argue that even those patients who receive deep vein thrombosis prophylaxis do, on occasions, go on to develop a deep vein thrombosis.

There have now been three important consensus conferences – one organised by the National Institute of Health, Bethesda, Washington in 1986, the second, organised in the UK, by THRIFT (a thrombosis risk assessment group) in 1992, and a European consensus conference, again, organised in the UK in 1992 – which made very clear recommendations. The recommendations of all three consensus groups include recommendations that all patients entering hospital should be assessed for the risk of deep vein thrombosis. Those patients with moderate risk of deep vein thrombosis should be considered for subcutaneous heparin and/or mechanical methods of prophylaxis. In the light of these recommendations, those patients considered to be at high risk of developing a deep vein thrombosis should now receive deep vein thrombosis prophylaxis.

# PULMONARY EMBOLISM

Pulmonary embolism occurs when solid material from the veins travels via the veins, through the heart and lodges in the pulmonary vessels. The majority of pulmonary emboli are caused by clotted blood, although some tumours, for example, kidney tumours, also embolise via the venous system. When a blood clot arrives in the lung, it will become trapped. Blood from the right side of the heart travels via the pulmonary artery into the lungs. A clot will become lodged when it is too large to travel through the vessels, which get progressively smaller as one goes deeper into the lungs. A large clot will completely occlude the circulation to the lung; this will result in the heart stopping. Smaller clots may just block a segment of the lung. This segment then collapses, before the lung tissue itself finally dies. Small clots cause wedge-shaped pulmonary infarcts (areas of lung death). These are usually associated with pleuritic chest pain (pain on breathing) and shortness of breath. The classic signs of a pulmonary embolism are acute onset of shortness of breath, coughing up blood (haemoptysis) and pleuritic chest pain. There may or may not be signs of a deep vein thrombosis in the lower legs. Just like deep vein thrombosis, the diagnosis of pulmonary embolism on clinical grounds alone can be extremely difficult. The differential diagnosis of a pulmonary embolism includes pneumonia and a variety of other lung conditions. If the diagnosis of pulmonary embolism is suspected, the patient should undergo further investigations. A chest X-ray may be helpful but, often, the appearances on chest X-ray are entirely normal. An electrocardiogram may show signs of right heart strain, suggesting a diagnosis of pulmonary embolism. The best way of making the diagnosis of pulmonary embolism is pulmonary arteriography. This used to involve injecting dye into the pulmonary artery and taking X-ray pictures. It is now possible to perform pulmonary arteriography using a digital subtraction technique (see Chapter 5). Once the diagnosis of pulmonary embolism has been made, treatment should be instituted. By taking samples of arterial blood and analysing the amount of oxygen and carbon dioxide, it is possible to see whether the patient's condition is improving and also possible to see when further small, often asymptomatic, emboli occur, indicating that the treatment may not be effective.

*Case*

## Deep vein thrombosis, pulmonary embolism and bleeding complications

A middle aged lady presented to the accident and emergency department with a history of a shortness of breath and chest pain. She had a past history of a deep vein thrombosis and pulmonary embolism, treated by intravenous heparin and the insertion of an inferior vena cava filter. She had also undergone a mastectomy for carcinoma of the breast. She was admitted to hospital. A diagnosis of deep vein thrombosis and further pulmonary embolism was made and she received intravenous heparin treatment. No investigations were carried out following her admission on the Wednesday. The following Tuesday she developed pain in the right leg followed by a weakness. A diagnosis of retroperitoneal haematoma was made. A ventilation perfusion scan which was carried out showed no evidence of a pulmonary embolism and the heparin was stopped. The plaintiff's case was that, following her admission on Wednesday, arrangements should have been made for her to undergo a venogram and a ventilation perfusion scan on Thursday or, by the latest, Friday. The presence of an inferior vena cava filter made it unlikely that she had a pulmonary embolism, although it could not be excluded. If the diagnosis of no pulmonary embolism had been made on Thursday or Friday, the heparin would have been stopped and she would not have gone on to develop a retroperitoneal haematoma.

The plaintiff argued that there was an unreasonable delay in carrying out the investigations, which led to prolonged heparinisation and a retroperitoneal haematoma.

In his judgment, the judge found that, although a delay of seven days or more would have been unreasonable, a delay of six days was not, and he found for the defendants.

## Case

### Injury to leg, followed by deep vein thrombosis

A young man was involved in a road traffic accident. He was riding a motorbike when he collided with a car. He was taken from the scene of the accident to an accident and emergency department in a hospital at 10 pm. The injuries he sustained involved a laceration to his left knee and a small laceration to his chin. He had no head injury, and the significant injury was a 15 cm laceration over the anterior aspect of his left knee. This was a deep laceration, down to the patella, with muscles and other structures exposed in the base of the wound. X-rays taken at the time showed no bony injury, and clinical examination of the knee joint showed no injury to the ligaments. X-rays were also taken of his skull and spine, to exclude fractures. Under a general anaesthetic the following day, his chin laceration was cleaned and sutured. His wound over the knee was debrided, irrigated and closed primarily with two layers of sutures. Following this, he was put into an above knee plaster cast and remained in hospital for four days. Two days following his discharge, he was admitted with an acutely swollen leg. Clinical diagnosis of a deep vein thrombosis was made and this was confirmed by venography. A clot was noted in the calf veins below the knee. He was fully anticoagulated with heparin, then switched to warfarin and remained hospitalised for a further eight days. He was discharged home with a support bandage and continued to attend physiotherapy for further period of six weeks.

One year after the accident, the patient was seen in hospital and underwent a formal non-invasive venous assessment. The non-invasive venous assessment confirmed a previous deep vein thrombosis and persisting reflux. Although the patient had no physical signs suggestive of a post-thrombotic limb, the non-invasive venous assessment confirmed deep vein damage. Given the presence of deep vein damage, the patient is at an increased risk of developing a further deep vein thrombosis and is probably at risk of developing a post-thrombotic limb.

On the basis of this investigation, the defendants offered £20,000 in settlement. This was accepted.

This case illustrates the importance of non-invasive vascular assessments in determining the extent of the problem and giving an indication of prognosis.

## Case

### Leg injury, superficial thrombophlebitis leading to deep vein thrombosis and fatal pulmonary embolism

A middle aged man suffered a minor soft tissue injury to his left leg. This was investigated by an X-ray and treated with a bandage. Because of the tightness of the bandage, he returned to casualty five days later complaining of pain in the shin. Another X-ray of the shin bones was normal. He subsequently developed a superficial thrombophlebitis, which initially responded to his general practitioner's treatment with butazolidin (an anti-inflammatory) and penbritin (antibiotics). However, he relapsed and these were stopped. He was referred to hospital, where a diagnosis of superficial thrombophlebitis affecting the long saphenous vein was made.

He was operated on on the same day and underwent a left sapheno-femoral ligation. At operation, an extensive clot was noted in the left saphenous vein. He was discharged the same day with pain tablets, but not anticoagulated.

He returned to his general practitioner two weeks later but suffered a massive, fatal pulmonary embolism while waiting in the doctor's surgery. Attempts at resuscitation were unsuccessful. Post mortem revealed a massive pulmonary embolus.

Even minor soft tissue injuries can lead to deep vein thrombosis. Any patient complaining of pain and swelling in the legs should be investigated for a possible deep vein thrombosis. When this patient complained of superficial thrombophlebitis, the possibility of an underlying deep vein problem should have been considered. If that problem had been considered and he had received anticoagulation, he would not have gone on to develop a fatal pulmonary embolism.

In this case, the failure to appreciate the importance of deep vein thrombosis and a failure to follow up the patient adequately led to his fatal pulmonary embolus. Had this patient received appropriate treatment, he would not have died.

This case settled at the court door with a payment of £20,000 plus the plaintiff's costs. The value of this case had been reduced because the plaintiff had an extremely poor work record, was not working before the injury and would probably not have worked following the injury.

## Case

*Road traffic accident with multiple injuries, deep vein thrombosis and pulmonary embolism*

A middle aged man was involved in a road traffic accident. He was driving, and was involved in a head-on collision with another vehicle, which turned in front of him. He was wearing a seat belt and, during the accident, sustained bruising to his chest and a fracture of the left calcaneum. He was taken to hospital, his left ankle was placed in a plaster of Paris backslab and he was admitted overnight for analgesia, being allowed home the following day. He was subsequently reviewed in the fracture clinic under the care of a consultant orthopaedic surgeon; the fractured calcaneum eventually healed, though with gross restriction of movement associated with a painful, stiff ankle joint, despite intensive physiotherapy. On review, it was decided that the subtalar joint should be fused.

The patient was then re-admitted to hospital to undergo subtalar joint arthrodesis the same day by a locum consultant orthopaedic surgeon. The operation note records no problems; the following day, the patient went into acute urinary retention, requiring catheterisation, but appears to have made an otherwise uneventful recovery and was allowed home one week later. He was then re-admitted two weeks later for change of plaster and removal of sutures, performed under general anaesthetic. The patient was allowed home the same day. He attended the accident and emergency department one month later, complaining of right sided chest pain associated with difficulty in breathing. He was thought to have a possible deep vein thrombosis with pulmonary embolism and was admitted under the care of a consultant physician. Intravenous heparin was commenced, and a ventilation/perfusion scan performed three days after admission. This showed mismatched perfusion defects in the middle lobe, unlikely for a pulmonary embolism, though, in view of the good history, anticoagulation was continued. The patient was subsequently commenced on warfarin and he was allowed home one week after admission. He was then reviewed one month later, at the request of his general practitioner, with a two day history of pleuritic left sided chest pain. He was clinically well, fully anticoagulated, reassured and sent home.

He continued to attend the orthopaedic department and was referred to a consultant haematologist, who noted that a hypercoagulable screen showed no abnormality; the last available note records his review by the consultant orthopaedic surgeon two years after the accident, when he noted that he had had symptoms of Sudeck's syndrome, which were gradually resolving, and that further review would be arranged for six months' time.

This man sustained serious injuries. His injuries included an orthopaedic injury and, of more significance, he went on to develop a deep vein thrombosis and pulmonary embolism. Although he has made a good recovery following his orthopaedic injuries, he is still left with a post-thrombotic limb. This has restricted his ability to move and has left him with a significant disability. He is disadvantaged with regard to employment.

Liability for the accident and subsequent problems has been accepted. Quantum is yet to be agreed.

## Treatment of pulmonary embolism

Before initiating treatment, it is normal practice to make the diagnosis. Sometimes, a pulmonary embolism can be very sudden and may, indeed, result in the heart stopping. When this happens, cardiopulmonary resuscitation should be started immediately. External cardiac massage sometimes results in the clots breaking up and being distributed to the periphery of the lungs. This may be sufficient to allow the heart to restart. With smaller emboli, treatment can be initiated with anticoagulants. In a patient who has had a pulmonary embolism but who has maintained their blood pressure and a reasonable pulse, intravenous heparin should be started. If the patient has a low blood pressure and is clearly showing signs of shock, then dissolution of the clot, using a fibrinolytic agent, that is, streptokinase, urokinase or plasminogen activator, should be carried out. In extreme cases, surgical removal of the clot can be carried out. Unless the patient is in a hospital with cardiac surgery facilities, the chances of successfully carrying out a pulmonary embolectomy are remote. If it is possible to get the patient to the operating theatre and open the chest, then removal of clot can be done surgically. The time available to do this can be measured in minutes and, therefore, the procedure is seldom carried out successfully. As with deep vein thrombosis, it is better to prevent pulmonary embolism than to treat it.

If a patient responds to either intravenous heparin or the fibrinolytic agents, treatment should be continued. Once the patient's condition begins to improve they may be started on oral anticoagulants. It is normal practice to continue the oral anticoagulants for between four and six months. If there is an underlying pre-disposing cause, no further investigations will be required. If the patient is young or there were no precipitating factors, then the patient should be screened for underlying clotting abnormalities.

# POST-THROMBOTIC LIMB

The post-thrombotic limb follows a deep vein thrombosis. A post-thrombotic syndrome takes, on average, 10 years to develop from the initial vein damage. The condition is characterised by swelling, pain, a feeling of heaviness and skin discolouration, the skin initially becoming red and then turning brown. The skin then becomes thickened (lipodermatosclerosis) and, finally, the patient may develop an ulcer. In a normal patient, walking is brought about by muscle contractions. As the muscles contract, the veins are compressed;. the presence of valves in the veins allows the blood to be forced back to the heart. In a patient with normally functioning valves, walking therefore results in a reduction of venous pressure. If the valves are damaged when the vein is compressed, blood is forced both up and down the leg. Forcing the blood down the leg results in the venous pressure being maintained or increased. As a result of this maintained venous pressure (venous hypertension), fluid and cells leak from the capillaries into the surrounding tissues. This initiates a reaction within the tissues, which leads to the deposition of fibrin and the activation of white blood cells. This process then leads on to scarring and skin breakdown, leading to ulceration. A patient who has had a deep vein thrombosis may complain that their leg feels heavy. They will notice the symptoms get worse if they stand a great deal. They will find it difficult to walk great distances and may end up performing a sedentary rather than an active job. The appearances of the leg may cause some concern. Currently treatment involves wearing a heavy elastic compression stocking. Attempts at repairing deep vein valves have been tried but the results are, overall, disappointing. If the patient goes on to develop an ulcer, they will require frequent dressings. Ulcers can be extremely painful, although the pain is usually associated with infection. Once a patient develops an ulcer, they will require frequent dressings and may require admission to hospital for surgical debridement of the wound, followed by split skin grafting.

Given that some deep vein thromboses are silent, a patient may not appreciate that they have ever had a deep vein thrombosis until they go on to develop the signs of a post-thrombotic syndrome. This may occur 10 years after their deep vein thrombosis and, in many instances, the association between a previous accident and the development of a post-thrombotic syndrome may not be recognised.

Any patient who sustains a serious injury to the leg or who has had serious illnesses may have had a silent deep vein thrombosis. This fact should be borne in mind when assessing patients following trauma to the legs, as it may have a significant effect on long term damages.

CHAPTER 10

# VARICOSE VEINS

## INTRODUCTION

Varicose veins are one of the commonest medical conditions. Thirty per cent of the adult population will suffer from varicose veins or varicose vein-related problems. Varicose veins affect men and women, although women tend to present at an earlier age, the veins often being precipitated by pregnancy. Because women wear skirts,they are four times more likely to complain and seek advice about treatment than men. When men present with varicose veins, they are usually of a long standing nature and often associated with quite marked skin changes.

Varicose veins are tortuous dilated superficial veins. They range from small spidery veins, through slightly larger reticular veins, to very large veins which may appear like bunches of grapes and which, if untreated, may bleed. Patients with varicose veins will present in one of two ways or, commonly, with a combination of both. The appearance of the veins bothers many people and many patients will present primarily concerned about the cosmetic appearance. Other patients are less concerned about the appearance but complain of the symptoms. The symptoms of varicose veins include pain, swelling, aching, discomfort, restlessness, itching, tingling and cramps. Not all patients will have all symptoms and the symptoms will not necessarily be present all the time. Although a patient may come complaining of symptoms, they are seldom satisfied unless they have a good overall functional and cosmetic result. Varicose veins seldom present as a life threatening condition and the majority of patients will come to no harm if they receive no treatment. A few patients burst varicose veins, or go on to develop venous ulceration simply due to their varicose veins, and these patients should be advised to undergo treatment.

It follows, therefore, that, in the majority of patients, one treatment option is to do nothing. A second treatment option involves the use of elastic compression stockings. The stockings do not improve the condition but they may stop the veins getting worse and give good symptomatic relief.

The majority of patients in the UK are treated by either injection treatment (sclerotherapy) or surgical treatment, or a combination of sclerotherapy and surgery. Despite being one of the commonest medical conditions, the treatment of varicose veins is often delegated to extremely junior doctors. Treatment of varicose veins by unsupervised juniors is probably not acceptable. The decision whether to treat a patient by surgery or by sclerotherapy should be made following a careful clinical assessment. In general, patients with severe varicose veins are better treated surgically, with sclerotherapy reserved for the treatment of patients with less severe varicosities or for the treatment of residual veins following prior surgery.

## ASSESSMENT OF PATIENTS WITH VARICOSE VEINS

Whilst the majority of patients with varicose veins undergo treatment without any formal assessment, there are an increasing number of centres which routinely perform a non-invasive venous assessment. Any patient presenting with recurrent varicose veins or complex varicose veins should routinely undergo a formal non-invasive venous assessment.

A patient presenting with varicose veins will have a history elicited, followed by a clinical examination. A clinical examination should be carried out with the patient standing. The leg is inspected from the front and back. The presence or absence of palpable veins in the groin and behind the knee is noted. By laying the patient on a couch and elevating the limb, all the veins should empty. Application of a tourniquet below the groin, above the knee and below the knee provides a very simple assessment of whether the patient has superficial venous reflux. If the varicose veins are controlled by simple tourniquets, then surgical treatment is probably indicated. More information can be obtained by a simple hand held Doppler ultrasound stethoscope and even more information obtained by the use of duplex ultrasound imaging. If there is evidence of junctional incompetence or large truncal varicosities, ligation of the junction and removal of the superficial veins provides a very effective and very good long term treatment. Where there is no junctional incompetence and no truncal reflux, varicosities can be treated effectively by sclerotherapy.

## SURGICAL TREATMENT OF VARICOSE VEINS

The surgical treatment of varicose veins is one of the most commonly performed surgical procedures. The majority of patients currently waiting to have surgery are waiting to undergo varicose vein surgery. Prior to carrying out varicose vein surgery, the patient should be assessed. This assessment will involve a clinical examination and may involve a formal non-invasive venous assessment. Before embarking upon the surgery, it is important that the patient fully understands the purpose of the operation, what is involved, what the potential problems are likely to be and what sort of outcome can be expected. A brief description of the surgical procedure should be given in terms that the patient is likely to understand. The operation is usually carried out with a full general anaesthetic, although local anaesthesia can be used for relatively minor cases. With the patient asleep and the leg slightly elevated to drain blood from the superficial veins, junctional incompetence is treated. There are two principal junctions – one in the groin, the sapheno-femoral junction, and one behind the knee, the sapheno-popliteal junction. If these junctions are incompetent, an incision is made, the superficial vein identified and the junction ligated. To get a good result, it is important that the junction is dissected carefully and that all branches arising from the junction are identified and divided without causing damage to the main underlying veins. If branches are left, the condition will recur. Over-zealous dissection or failure to identify the anatomy properly can result in damage to the main deep vein. This is unacceptable and should not occur. Having divided the junction, the superficial vein should be removed. Whilst there is still debate as to whether the superficial vein should be removed or left in place, there is clear evidence emerging that leaving the vein is associated with a much higher recurrence rate. Those surgeons who advocate leaving the vein argue that it may be useful as an arterial conduit for arterial reconstruction. Those who believe that the long saphenous vein or the short saphenous vein should be removed argue that varicose veins make extremely poor grafts. When removing the long saphenous vein and short saphenous vein, they should be removed to just below the knee or to the mid calf. If the long saphenous vein is removed to the ankle (an old technique) or the short saphenous vein removed to the ankle (again, an old technique), the procedure is associated with a significant incidence of nerve injury.

These veins can be removed by passing a fine surgical instrument through the vein, tying it to the top of the vein and inverting it and removing it by a stripping technique. Any residual varicosities can be removed through 1.5 mm incisions. It is not necessary to make large incisions on the leg and not necessary to ligate the veins when they are being removed.

Prior to carrying out surgery, patients should be warned that their leg will be extensively bruised. Having removed the vein, bleeding occurs. This blood will initially set before being dissolved. The bruising will track to the surface and the leg will appear initially red, then a dark blue colour, before going greenish-yellow. The appearance of the leg will return to normal, but the patient will experience some lumpiness in the deeper layers, which clears over a six week period. Provided the patients have been warned about this, they accept it without complaint.

When making small incisions and removing veins, damage to small cutaneous nerves may occur, leaving small patches of numbness. Damage to major nerves remains unacceptable. By not stripping to the ankle, the incidence of saphenous nerve injury has been eliminated. Up to 10% of patients will experience small areas of numbness and tingling. It is relatively unusual for a patient to complain of a large area of numbness. Very large areas of numbness are associated with major sensory nerve damage. If this damage is caused at the time of surgery, that is probably unacceptable.

Unfortunately, some patients develop these signs and symptoms as a result of bruising. The bruising may surround the nerve, leading to either a temporary or, sometimes, quite a prolonged period of sensory loss. Most patients do not complain about the numbness but get extremely upset when the nerve begins to recover, as they experience a burning and tingling-like sensation. Damage to motor nerves, nerves that work the muscles, should not occur. Any patient left with weakness should, with some justification, complain that the treatment that they have received falls below an acceptable standard of care.

If, following varicose vein surgery, a patient complains of severe pain or shows signs of weakness, the incision should be explored. A nerve may have become incorporated in the closure and removal of the suture may alleviate the symptoms.

Damage to main arteries and veins should not occur. During the course of dissection, if the surgeon fails to identify the anatomy properly, accidental division or even stripping of main veins and main arteries has been known to occur. These injuries are always unacceptable and there can be no satisfactory defence. When major veins and arteries are damaged, early investigation and appropriate reconstructive surgery will minimise the damage.

*Case*

*Varicose veins, with sclerotherapy leading to superficial thrombophlebitis, deep vein thrombosis and fatal pulmonary embolism*

A 39 year old man was referred by his general practitioner, complaining of pain in his knee. The pain was attributed to superficial varicose veins, which were treated by sclerotherapy. Following this, he complained of pain and swelling in the leg. An erroneous diagnosis of superficial thrombophlebitis was made to account for the swelling, when, in fact, he had a deep vein thrombosis. The deep vein thrombosis subsequently extended and embolised, causing death.

The defendants denied liability. They argued that superficial thrombophlebitis was not a serious condition and not related to deep vein thrombosis. When the superficial thrombophlebitis extended up the leg and into the deep veins, the defendants successfully argued that this was such a rare complication that no reasonably competent doctor would have known about this problem. The defendants called in expert evidence to support their case. The judge found that localised swelling was consistent with superficial thrombophlebitis but, had the leg been generally swollen, then he would have found that there was deep vein thrombosis. If there were clinical signs of deep vein thrombosis, this should have been recognised and the plaintiff should have received treatment. The defendants were successful because of the rarity of the case and the fact that the plaintiff was unable to show that the leg was generally swollen.

The judge found in favour of the defendants.

*Case*

*Treatment for varicose veins, leading to sensory nerve damage*

A 24 year old woman with a three year history of varicose veins in her left leg was referred by her general practitioner to a consultant surgeon at a hospital. She was seen by a surgical registrar, who noted that she had quite marked varicosities in the left long saphenous vein system and over the back of the knee, with a few minimal varicosities on the medial aspect of her right knee. Her name was placed on the waiting list for a left high saphenous ligation, stripping and multiple ties. The long saphenous vein was removed from the groin to the ankle.

She saw her general practitioner in September 1990, when it was noted that she had undergone surgery for her varicose veins one week previously and the wounds were still sore, but that there were otherwise no problems with these. The patient was reviewed in the surgical out-patient clinic in February 1991, following varicose vein surgery. She complained of numbness and paraesthesia around the ankle. Examination revealed the groin wound to be healed with no residual varicose veins. She was reassured that the numbness was due to damage to the cutaneous nerve and would heal slowly. She was told there was no problem and was discharged.

Removal of the long saphenous vein to the ankle is associated with a significant incidence of saphenous nerve injury. For that reason, most surgeons have now stopped stripping the long saphenous vein to the ankle. This is well documented in the textbooks and it is now recommended that the long saphenous vein should not be removed beyond the mid calf. Removing it was considered to represent unacceptable medical practice.

The judge found in favour of the plaintiff and awarded damages of £7,000 plus costs.

# SCLEROTHERAPY

Sclerotherapy is injection treatment for varicose veins. Unlike surgical treatment, sclerotherapy can be carried out by any doctor at any location. The importance of adequate training, proper patient assessment, a good technique and proper follow up cannot be over-emphasised. The principle of sclerotherapy is to inject an irritant solution into a vein which has been emptied of blood. The irritant solution will then cause an inflammatory reaction, resulting in the destruction of the vein lining, leading to a fibrous obliteration of the vein. Being irritant, if the solution is injected outside the vein in large quantities, it will produce an extra-vascular reaction which may result in the skin breaking down and ulceration. Injection of a sclerosant into a full vein will result in a thrombophlebitis. This will produce a linear discolouration of the skin along the line of the vein and is associated with recanalisation and varicose vein recurrence. The first principle of successful sclerotherapy is good patient selection. Patients with junctional or significant truncal reflux should first undergo surgical treatment. An effective sclerosant which can be injected into an empty vein should be used. Having injected into an empty vein, compression should be applied to the vein to keep the vein walls approximated until a marked inflammatory response can be generated to cause endothelial disobliteration and total removal of the vein by the body's own defence mechanism. The concentration of sclerosant is important. If highly concentrated sclerosants are used in small vessels, a very marked inflammatory response can occur, which can cause damage to surrounding tissues. The principle, therefore, is the larger the vein, the more concentrated the sclerosant. Using dilute solutions of sclerosant, it is possible to inject dermal flares, the finest of varicose veins. Complications following sclerotherapy do occur and it is therefore important that patients fully understand these problems. When injecting the fine, thread-like veins, some degree of extravasation is inevitable. Provided a dilute solution is used and only a minor amount of extravasation occurs, there should be no problem. Occasionally, when injecting over the front of the leg or in the region of the ankle, organisms of the skin may get massaged into the injection site. If this is recognised and treated with antibiotics at the first sign of any redness, the condition settles. If no treatment is given, the redness may expand to give a small black ulcer. These ulcers usually heal without leaving any long term scarring but, in the short term, can be extremely distressing.

If a large amount of sclerosant is given outside a vein when trying to inject into a large vein, then the skin may break down. Skin ulceration cannot be caused by sclerosant leaking back along the needle track. It only occurs when a significant quantity of sclerosant is injected in the wrong place.

Sometimes, the patient will complain of pain if the injection is given outside the vein but, because the sclerosant solutions are buffered to a neutral pH, pain is often not a feature and the first sign that the patient or the doctor will have that there is a problem is when the ulcer begins to develop.

When inserting a needle into the vein, it is important to make sure the needle is in the vein and to make sure that the technique employed ensures that the needle does not slip out of the vein. If, when injecting, there is resistance or any doubt about the position of the needle in relation to the vein, the injection should cease immediately, the leg should be returned to the dependent position and the needle re-inserted. It is a standard practice to insert the needle with the leg dependent and then elevate the limb to remove the blood. It is during this period of elevation that, if a poor technique is employed, the needle may come out of the vein.

Injecting large quantities of sclerosant in superficial veins can cause quite a marked thrombophlebitis, particularly if the vein is not emptied. This can result in the patient complaining of quite severe pain. If a patient does develop a superficial thrombophlebitis and then the superficial thrombophlebitis appears to extend, this patient must be observed carefully. If the superficial thrombophlebitis extends up the superficial veins towards the groin, surgical intervention should be carried out or, at the very least, the patient admitted to hospital for further assessment and treatment with anticoagulants.

If this rare but well recognised condition of rapidly ascending superficial thrombophlebitis is missed, the patient may go on to develop deep vein problems, which may result in pulmonary embolism and death.

When injecting the superficial veins, there is a small risk that the sclerosant material can travel directly through into the deep veins. The blood flow in the deep veins is usually such that it causes no problems. However, occasionally, there have been reports of thrombosis occurring in the deep veins. If a patient who has undergone sclerotherapy complains of swelling or discomfort in the leg, then further investigation should be carried out. The best investigation involves duplex ultrasound imaging. If there is any doubt about the diagnosis, this investigation should be repeated. It may be necessary to treat the patient with anticoagulants in the short term.

Following sclerotherapy, the leg is usually compressed with a bandage. This bandage may remain in place for as little as 24 hours or may be left on for as long as six weeks. There is very little scientific evidence to suggest how long these bandages should remain.

It is important, following sclerotherapy, that the patients are warned that, if they develop pain in their leg, and, in particular, if they feel the bandage is tight, they should seek medical advice. Normally, following the application of a bandage over a period of six to 12 hours, the bandage will lose its compression. If the patient complains that the bandage is getting tighter, then this usually suggests that the leg is swelling. Following routine sclerotherapy, there is very little swelling. Swelling may, therefore, indicate the development of a deep vein problem and this should be investigated.

## MICROSCLEROTHERAPY

Microsclerotherapy involves the same principles as sclerotherapy. Many patients present with superficial flares, sometimes referred to as spider veins or as dermal flares. These veins may be associated with proper varicose veins but, in two-thirds of cases, are unrelated. Microsclerotherapy involves the insertion of an extremely fine needle into one of these veins. Having inserted the needle into a vein, a very dilute solution of sclerosant is injected. As the sclerosant solution spreads through the flares, the veins seem to disappear. Following the disappearance, there is a slight reddening (erythematous change) that takes place. If blood leaks back into the veins, the vein walls themselves have been damaged and the veins will disappear over a three month period. Prior to carrying out this treatment, patients are usually advised that, sometimes, there is an instant improvement, but they may have to wait up to three months to see the benefits. Again, patients should be warned that there is a small risk that they may develop a local infection and that, if they do, they should seek immediate medical attention. This will avoid the development of a small ulcerated area. The treatment is entirely cosmetic and the treatment continues until the patient is entirely satisfied. As bigger clusters of veins are cleared, the patient complains about smaller ones. If there is an underlying vein problem this should be addressed before treating the superficial veins.

*Case*

## Varicose veins and development of skin ulceration

A 37 year old lady with varicose veins was referred to a consultant surgeon. She underwent sclerotherapy to both calves. When the dressing on the left leg was removed, it was noted that she had an ulcer over the left calf. This subsequently deteriorated and she consulted her general practitioner, who gave her a course of antibiotics. However, the ulcer was increasing in size, and the general practitioner arranged for review by a district nurse. The district nurse was unhappy with the state of the ulcer and the patient was referred back to the hospital. Curettage of the wound was undertaken; the wound was then packed and the patient was seen for daily dressings, being eventually discharged by the district nurse. She was seen four months later, when it was noted that the ulcer had healed and arrangements were made for further review in one year's time.

The plaintiff's case was that the doctor carrying out the injection technique (sclerotherapy) used an incorrect technique, which resulted in the breakdown of skin and her developing an ulcer. If the doctor had used a proper technique, this complication could have been avoided and she would not have suffered pain and would not have had residual scarring. The defendants argued that this was a recognised complication of sclerotherapy and that this complication could occur as a result of extravasation of sclerosant from the vein. The plaintiff's expert accepted that ulceration was a well reported complication but argued that it was one which only occurs when an incorrect technique is used. If the sclerosant material is injected into the vein (intravascularly), then skin ulceration cannot occur. Skin ulceration only occurs when a significant quantity of sclerosant is injected outside the vein and close to the skin surface. The literature supports the importance of making sure that the needle is in the vein when the injection occurs; whilst removal of the needle might result in some extravasation, the amount of extravasation is so small that it cannot cause sufficient damage to produce the degree of ulceration.

The judge found in favour of the plaintiff and awarded damages for pain, suffering and cosmetic disability of £11,000.

## ALTERNATIVE FORMS OF TREATMENT

The laser and a new form of treatment, high intensity light treatment (photoderm), are widely used in the treatment of cutaneous flares and arterio-venous malformations. The principle of treatment is coagulation with both laser light and high intensity filtered light being absorbed by red tissues selectively, causing thermal damage. There are specific indications for the use of laser and for the use of high intensity light treatment. Flares on the face respond well to high intensity light treatment. The laser has been used for the treatment of port wine stains and other arterio-venous malformations. More recently, photoderm is also being used in the same situation. The treatments may need to be applied on more than one occasion and, to avoid disappointment, patients should be given a realistic expectation of what they can expect to achieve and when that achievement might be reached.

# CHAPTER 11

# VENOUS AND ARTERIAL RECONSTRUCTION

## VENOUS TRAUMA

The veins may be injured as a result of direct penetrating injuries (stabbings), they may injured indirectly when fractures of the long bones occur, or they may be damaged during the course of an operation.

Any injury to a vein may be associated with considerable bleeding. There are a large number of veins and damage to veins, once the bleeding has been controlled, may present no clinical problems. The larger the vein, the more likely the patient is to suffer long term problems. Arterial injuries (page 113) are usually recognised early, and surgical repair is carried out. The importance of co-existing venous injuries has been recognised and primary surgical repair of the veins is now carried out, particularly when the injury includes a large vein (femoral vein, iliac vein, etc). Failure to recognise a co-existing venous injury may result in early failure of an arterial reconstruction for trauma. Veins are very thin-walled and extremely friable. A penetrating injury to a vein may result in a long laceration. Simple ligation of the vein may be adequate distally but, where the vein has a large diameter, repair should be carried out. Surgical repair of venous injury is technically more difficult than that of arterial injury. Blood tends to spurt from arterial injuries, and the source is quite obvious. The blood in the veins is at a low pressure and tends to well up, making it extremely difficult to identify the site of injury. Pressure on the vein above and below the site of injury accompanied by good suction to remove the blood will allow adequate visualisation. It may be possible to suture a vein to close a hole. It may be necessary to insert a patch or, in some instances, it may be necessary to replace a whole segment. By removing superficial veins (for example, the saphenous vein, if it is available), it is possible to make both the short segment graft and patches.

Following venous repair, thrombosis may occur. To prevent thrombosis, the patient may be heparinised or be provided with an intermittent compression device to squeeze blood through the veins to keep them patent. Other techniques sometimes employed include connecting a small branch in an artery directly into a vein to increase blood flow (arterio-venous fistula). This is a temporary procedure and, once the repair has fully healed, the fistula can be closed.

*Case*

*Treatment for varicose veins, leading to injury to deep veins*

A 48 year old woman with varicose veins involving both legs was referred by her general practitioner to hospital. She was seen by a locum consultant surgeon, who noted that she had bilateral sapheno-femoral junction reflux, together with left short saphenous vein reflux, and her name was to be placed on the waiting list for ligation of these vessels.

She was subsequently admitted to the hospital. The operation was performed by a registrar, who started by exploring the left popliteal fossa. During the course of this, the popliteal vein was divided, together with part of an adjacent nerve. The registrar sought help and a consultant surgeon performed a vein interposition graft to the popliteal vein, using a length of short saphenous vein. The patient was subsequently anticoagulated with a heparin infusion, followed by oral warfarin.

Post-operatively, it was noted that she had developed a left foot drop with some sensory loss; the sensory loss gradually improved, but the patient still required a foot splint.

She was subsequently reviewed in clinic and continued with physiotherapy. Nerve conduction studies were performed, which recorded that she had a lesion of the lateral popliteal nerve and partial involvement of the posterior tibial nerve with evidence of re-enervation.

When last seen, the patient had regained sensation, but still had a degree of foot drop.

Surgery to the popliteal fossa is complicated. Pre-operative duplex ultrasound scanning identifies the anatomy. This is helpful in all cases, but essential in those patients undergoing recurrent surgery.

Damage to major nerves and to veins is unacceptable. Damage to the popliteal vein in this case was recognised and surgical repair was carried out. Although the injury to the vein undoubtedly delayed the patient's discharge from hospital, there are no long term consequences with regard to the circulation.

During the course of this operation, however, a major motor nerve was damaged and this led to weakness. There has been partial recovery and this has reduced the amount of damages.

The patient still has varicose veins and still requires further surgery.

Although liability was never admitted, the case settled for £15,000 plus costs.

## Case

*Treatment for varicose veins, leading to injury to deep veins (bilateral)*

A 46 year old man underwent injection sclerotherapy to varicose veins in his left leg in 1973, followed by ligation to veins in 1978. In 1988, he had further problems with varicose veins in both legs and was referred to a consultant surgeon. He was seen in clinic and his name was placed on the waiting list for right high saphenous ligation, ligation of perforators in the right leg and ligation of recurrent perforators in the left leg. However, when admitted to hospital, it appears that the intention was to carry out bilateral high saphenous ligation with stripping. Surgery was performed by the consultant surgeon and his registrar, the operation note appearing to indicate that bilateral high saphenous ligation and stripping was attempted but, during the procedure, the femoral vein on both sides was damaged, requiring the interposition of an 8 mm PTFE (polytetralfluoroethylene) graft by the vascular surgeon on call. Post-operatively, the patient was commenced on heparin infusion and, subsequently, on warfarin. He was gradually mobilised and discharged home. He was subsequently reviewed in the out-patient clinic, where it was noted that he complained of persistent low back pain, for which he was referred to the rheumatologists. He also complained of pain in both groins, although no abnormality could be found, and he was finally discharged from surgical follow up. He appears subsequently to have seen an orthopaedic surgeon about pain in his hips, but has also been discharged from his care.

Damage to the femoral vein during varicose vein surgery is unacceptable. The mistake here was to pass the stripper from the ankle to the groin. The stripper passed from the superficial vein into the deep veins in the mid thigh region. When the stripper was removed, a segment of deep vein was removed with it. This was recognised at the time of surgery and the patient underwent a successful reconstruction.

Despite undergoing a successful reconstruction, which, on non-invasive venous testing, appears to be functioning normally, the patient is unable to work.

The hospital has admitted liability but disputed quantum. This case is currently being discussed. It is probable that the patient will be compensated for pain and suffering and for some limitation in his ability to work.

## Valve repair/replacement

Damage to venous valves occurs with ageing and following thrombosis. As the vein walls stretch, the valve cusps become floppy and leak. This will lead to changes in the microcirculation, resulting in skin changes and, potentially, venous ulceration. If the valves are damaged by clotting again, the same changes will occur. Primary valve repair for non-thrombotic disease can be carried out. This operation involves tightening the valve cusps. The procedure depends on having valves that are floppy but have not been affected by thrombosis. These procedures are only suitable for a small number of patients and the results are unpredictable; therefore, patients should be fully informed as to the nature of surgery and the fact that it may not work.

It is possible to remove functioning valves from the arm and place them in the leg in an attempt to improve the venous circulation. Again, these procedures are experimental and the results unpredictable. These procedures are usually reserved for patients with very severe disease and then only carried out when the patient has a full understanding of the nature of the operation, the potential benefits and the long term complications.

## Venous bypass surgery

Some patients are left with a permanent obstruction to the deep veins following a deep vein thrombosis. If the obstruction occurs in the ileo femoral segment, small collateral channels will develop to take blood from the leg back into the central circulation. Sometimes these channels are not adequate, and when the patient exercises, the venous pressure in the leg increases and the patient complains of a bursting sensation in the calf. Many patients who have an isolated venous thrombosis affecting the veins in the pelvis (ileo femoral segment) have normal valvular function in the rest of the leg. These patients respond well to venous bypass surgery. The block can be bypassed by taking a venous graft from above the block to below the block. The best graft material includes the patient's own superficial veins. If these are not available, synthetic material can be used.

A very simple but effective operation involves taking the long saphenous vein from the good leg. The vein is detached just above the knee and, through multiple separate incisions, all the branches are divided. The vein is left attached to the femoral vein and then tunnelled across the lower abdomen to be inserted into the femoral vein on the affected side. This allows blood travelling up the obstructed leg to be diverted across the lower abdomen into the veins draining the normal leg. This operation (Palma operation) is an extremely effective surgical procedure, relieving obstructed symptoms following venous occlusion. If the patient complains of bursting sensation on exercise, this operation will probably relieve the symptoms. The operation is not so effective in reducing leg swelling.

Before carrying out these procedures, it is important to assess the patient fully. This will include an examination with duplex ultrasound imaging and may also include investigations to measure the venous pressure. In a normal patient, on exercise, venous pressure drops. In a patient who has valvular dysfunction, the venous pressure will not drop and, in a patient who has venous outflow obstruction, the venous pressure will increase on exercise.

## ARTERIAL TRAUMA

Injuries to arteries are common. They may be associated with sharp trauma (stabbing), associated with orthopaedic injuries or associated with other surgical procedures, including laparoscopy. Unlike veins, there is usually one artery supplying an area of the body – the femoral artery supplies the leg, the axillary artery supplies the arm, the renal artery supplies the kidney, etc. Damage to an artery will result in either complete or partial interruption to the area supplied. Early recognition, proper investigations and appropriate management are essential. The treatment of arterial injuries is urgent and treatment should be carried out within a few hours of presentation. Sometimes, the presentation is obvious and blood may be seen to be spurting from a wound; on other occasions, the diagnosis only becomes apparent when the patient is examined. All patients presenting with injuries to the limb should be properly examined. The presence or absence of pulses should be recorded, along with any sensory or motor nerve deficits.

The signs of an arterial injury include pallor, coldness, numbness, loss of sensation and absent pulses. Pulses may be difficult to feel in patients who have lost a considerable amount of blood and, if there is doubt about the presence of an arterial injury, a Doppler stethoscope should initially be used. If doubt about the presence of a vascular injury remains, duplex ultrasound imaging or arteriography should be carried out. Arterial injuries may occur when a limb is injured. Dislocation of a joint may result in the artery being stretched, the lining being damaged and occlusion occurring. When the patient is seen in the casualty department, the dislocation may already have been reduced, but the damage to the artery remains. When a bone fractures, a spike may penetrate the artery, causing damage. The artery may also suffer contusion or twisting during the course of a fracture. Following the fracture of a long bone, there is considerable bleeding and this may cause compression. The limbs are surrounded by an inelastic sleeve and, if there is significant bleeding beneath this, the pressure increases and the patient will develop a compartment syndrome. A compartment syndrome occurs when the vessels within that compartment become compressed and the blood supply then becomes inadequate. Unless this condition is recognised and treated by releasing the compartment, the muscles will die.

It follows, therefore, that any patient who has been injured should be examined fully and that examination should include checking the circulation.

## Management of a patient with an arterial injury

When an arterial injury is suspected, urgent investigations and treatment should be carried out. With multiple injuries, it is necessary to prioritise the injuries, dealing first with breathing, then with bleeding complications, the brain and, finally, the bones. With an arterial injury, it is necessary to stop the bleeding to determine the extent of the injury and then to affect a repair, with restoration of the circulation. Bleeding can be controlled by pressure, blood loss can be replaced by transfusion and the nature and extent of the damage assessed by duplex ultrasound imaging or arteriography. Sometimes, the extent of the injury is clear and direct surgical repair can be carried out without the need for investigations.

Surgery may involve simple suturing of an artery, patching the artery or replacing a segment of artery.

Having completed the surgical procedure, if there has been a delay of more than one and a half hours before restoration of the circulation, then the fascial covering of each compartment should be divided, in order to prevent the development of a compartment syndrome. At the end of the surgical procedure, it is important to check that the circulation has been adequately restored. The return of pulses, either palpable or audible on Doppler, will provide a useful indicator. These pulses should then be observed, initially on a half hourly basis and then on an hourly basis, before reducing to four hourly, to make sure that there is no late occlusion of the artery.

Once the arterial circulation has been restored to the limb, the patient should receive treatment for other injuries. Sometimes, it is convenient to fix the bones prior to carrying out the arterial reconstruction. If there is likely to be a significant delay, or the operation to fix the bones is complicated, then arterial reconstruction should be carried out, or arterial bypass performed, to preserve the tissues in the limb.

# APPENDIX I

# MEDICO-LEGAL ASSESSMENT OF THE VASCULAR PATIENT

The majority of vascular patients will present to their solicitors when they experience an unexpected outcome. That unexpected outcome may involve the loss of the limb, an abnormality of limb function or a poor cosmetic result. Whilst the loss of the limb may be the inevitable consequence of the underlying disease process, there are many situations where the loss of the limb can be directly attributed to the action or lack of action of the patient's medical attendants. The initial assessment will involve identifying the presenting problem. Although some patients will treat themselves initially, they usually present to their general practitioner or the accident and emergency department if the signs and symptoms are getting worse. It is the thoroughness of the initial assessment which needs to be examined:

(a) was a proper examination of the circulation carried out?

(b) was this information recorded in the notes?

(c) what advice was the patient given?

(d) what treatment did the patient receive? and

(e) was he/she advised to return for a follow up visit?

There are situations where a patient's condition can improve, remain the same or deteriorate. A period of conservative management, that, waiting and seeing, may be appropriate if the patient's condition is improving or remaining the same. If the patient's condition is deteriorating or has not improved, then further investigation and treatment are essential.

The point at which a patient is referred for a specialist opinion will depend on the severity of the underlying condition and the rapidity of progress. Arteriosclerosis is a slowly progressive condition but acute occlusion due to a thrombosis or embolisation can occur. Whilst it might be reasonable practice to make a routine out-patient appointment for a patient complaining of intermittent claudication at a hundred yards, a patient complaining of severe pain in the leg which has suddenly become pulseless and pale requires an immediate referral. A patient with severe arterial insufficiency, with or without infection, needs an extremely urgent out-patient appointment. A vascular opinion can be obtained the same day and, in urgent cases, it is unsatisfactory to rely on a normal appointment system.

Delays may be caused by the patient's failure to present to a doctor, the failure of the doctor to carry out an proper initial assessment and refer the patient, and the failure to be seen at the hospital.

Whether these delays are critical will clearly depend on the underlying problems. In assessing the hospital management, the thoroughness of the initial clinical investigation and of the notes should be assessed. Having completed the investigations, a treatment plan should be effected. The treatment plan should follow reasonable guidelines. Experimental procedures should be clearly documented and discussed with the patient. During any treatment, the patient should be monitored for signs of deterioration. When there are signs of deterioration, the treatment should be changed or reasons why the treatment is not being changed recorded. When the patient is admitted to hospital, it is important to record the presence or absence of pulses in both limbs and the blood pressure needs to be recorded. Some simple non-invasive tests, such as Doppler examination of the pulses, should also be undertaken. An assessment of the limb viability should be made and recorded. In an acutely ischaemic limb, further investigations, including Duplex ultrasound imaging and arteriography, should then be carried out without undue delay.

Having carried out the investigations, the results of these investigations need to be recorded and actions taken. Appropriate surgical treatment may then follow. In assessing these cases, the only information available is the surgeon's operation note. Most of these notes will record the standard surgical procedure. A surgeon may record specific difficulties and variations from the normal surgical procedure. The fuller the operation note and the more details provided, the more difficult it is to criticise the surgeon. A full assessment of the post-operative monitoring should be undertaken. Following any vascular reconstruction a number of questions arise:

(a) were the pulses in the limb monitored post-operatively?

(b) did these pulses disappear?

(c) was this information relayed to the doctors?

(d) what action was taken?

(e) were antibiotics prescribed to cover the operation?

(f) how long were they continued for?

(g) was heparin prescribed to prevent thrombosis? and

(h) was it continued into the post-operative period?

Complications occur following any surgical procedure and will be recorded in both the operating notes and the nursing kardex (record). Complications, such as post-operative pyrexia, wound infections, urinary tract infections and respiratory infections, are common. Unexpected complications may also arise, including excessive bleeding and graft thrombosis. If these complications occurred, what, if any, action was taken?

Finally, the question of causation needs to be addressed at an early stage. This is particularly important with patients being treated for arterial insufficiency. This is a progressive condition with progressive hardening and narrowing of the arteries. Even in the best hands, medical intervention can only delay the onset of this condition. Whilst errors may occur in the assessment and medical management, these errors need to alter the outcome significantly before incurring further costs.

# APPENDIX II

# GLOSSARY OF TERMS

**A**

| | |
|---|---|
| Angiography | An imaging process, involving the injection of radio-opaque contrast material into vessels to outline them, followed by an X-ray |
| Angioplasty | Stretching an artery with a balloon catheter |
| ABPI | Ankle brachial pressure index |
| Aorta | The main artery leaving the heart and running throughout the abdominal cavity. |
| Arteriotomy | Making a hole in an artery |
| Arteriovenous malformation | An abnormal group of arteries and veins |
| Artery | A vessels taking blood from the heart to the limbs and organs |
| Autogenous saphenous vein | The patient's own saphenous vein, removed and inserted into the arterial system as a conduit |
| Axillary artery | The artery supplying blood to the upper limbs |

**B**

| | |
|---|---|
| Baro receptors | Receptors in circulation which monitor pressure |
| Brachial pulse | A pulse felt at the elbow |

**C**

| | |
|---|---|
| Carotid artery | The artery supplying the brain |
| Carotid pulse | A pulse felt midway in between the supra-sternal notch and the base of the earlobe |
| Claudicating distance | The distance a patient can walk before incurring pain. This distance is constant. When the pain occurs, if the patient rests, the pain will go and the patient can walk a similar distance |

| | |
|---|---|
| Claudication | Pain which comes on in muscles during exercise when there is insufficient oxygen. As the oxygen is used up, anaerobic respiration (metabolism without oxygen) occurs, leading to an increase in lactic acid and pain |
| Clot | Blood setting to become solid |
| Colour Duplex ultrasound | Based on a Duplex ultrasound machine, colour Duplex enables the flow to be coloured red or blue, depending on whether it is flowing forwards or backwards |
| Critical ischaemia | A blood supply to the limb that is so poor, the limb's viability is threatened |

## D

| | |
|---|---|
| Dacron | Synthetic material woven or knitted into a graft |
| DVT | Deep vein thrombosis |
| Degenerative changes | The breakdown of normal structure |
| Diabetes | An abnormality of sugar metabolism |
| DSA | Digital subtraction angiography |
| Doppler stethoscope | Used to measure flow through a vessel using the Doppler shift principle, whereby sound alters its frequency, and, hence, the audible note changes, when it is reflected from a moving or flowing surface |
| Dorsalis pedis pulse | A pulse felt on the front of the foot, midway between the first and second toe and the central point of the ankle |
| Duplex ultrasound | High frequency sound, which is reflected from tissues to build up a two dimensional picture, similar to radar, but combined with a device which can detect movement |

## E

| | |
|---|---|
| ECG | Electrocardiogram |
| Embolus | Solid material moving freely in the circulation until trapped |

## Glossary of Terms

| | |
|---|---|
| Endarterectomy | Removal of the inner layer from an artery to increase flow of blood |
| Endovascular prostheses | Grafts inserted via catheters within the lumen (keyhole vascular surgery) |

**F**

| | |
|---|---|
| False aneurysm | A swelling associated with a blood vessel containing blood, but no true arterial wall |
| Femoral pulse | Felt in the groin midway between the anterior/superior iliac spine and the symphysis pubis |
| Femoro-femoral crossover graft | A graft taking blood from one femoral artery, across the lower abdomen and into the other femoral artery |
| Fibrinolysis | Dissolution of fibrin, a major constituent of clot |

**H**

| | |
|---|---|
| Heparin | A naturally occurring anticoagulant |

**I**

| | |
|---|---|
| Iliac artery | Arises where the aorta divides into two to supply blood to the left and right limbs |
| In situ saphenous vein graft | Saphenous vein left in situ, disconnected from the venous system and used as an arterial conduit. The valves preventing flow in the opposite direction are disrupted |

**L**

| | |
|---|---|
| Lumen | The space inside an artery or vein |

**M**

| | |
|---|---|
| MRI | Magnetic resonance imaging |
| Microangiopathy | A disease process affecting the very small vessels |

## P

| | |
|---|---|
| Pallor | Paleness of the limb |
| Patent | Open |
| Percutaneous technique | A technique performed through the skin |
| Photoplethysmography | A method for measuring blood flow, involving light reflected from the skin affected by the amount of blood in the tissues |
| Popliteal pulse | A pulse felt at the back of the knee in the midline |
| PTFE | Polytetralfluoroethylene – a synthetic material used for grafts |
| Posterior tibial pulse | A pulse felt at the ankle behind and below the medial malleolus |
| Pulmonary artery | The artery taking the oxygenated blood from the heart to the lungs |
| PE | Pulmonary embolus – clot, usually travelling from the leg, pelvic vein or, occasionally, from the heart entering the pulmonary artery and becoming lodged in the lung |
| Pulmonary vein | The vein taking oxygenated blood from the lungs to the left side of the heart to be circulated around the body |
| Pulse | A point at which the blood flow through a vessel may be felt |

## R

| | |
|---|---|
| Radial pulse | A pulse felt at the wrist |
| Rest pain | Pain the limb which occurs without exercise. This pain usually occurs at the furthest point from the heart and is indicative of critical ischaemia |
| Reverse saphenous vein graft | A graft in which the saphenous vein has been removed and turned round to allow blood to flow in the opposite direction. The saphenous vein has valves which prevent the flow in the opposite direction. If the saphenous vein is left in situ, these valves have to be disrupted |

## Glossary of Terms

### S

| | |
|---|---|
| Sclerotherapy | Chemically controlled damage to the lining of the vein, in order to occlude it |
| Stenotic disease | A disorder in which the hardening of the arterial wall results in narrowing |
| Stent | A rigid tube made of wire or synthetic material, designed to keep the lumen open, following balloon dilatation |
| Strain gauge plethysmography | A method for measuring blood flow, which measures limb swelling in response to arterial inflow and venous outflow |
| SVT | Superficial vein thrombosis |

### T

| | |
|---|---|
| Thrombophlebitis | Inflammation of the vein with blood clot |
| Thrombus | A mixture of blood clot, platelets and fibrin |
| TPA | Tissue plasminogen activator – used to dissolve clot |
| TIA | Transient ischaemic attacks – a neurological event which lasts less than 24 hours |
| Trouser graft | Synthetic graft, shaped like a pair of trousers, used to bypass aorto-iliac obstructions |
| True aneurysm | Dilatation of a vessel |

### U

| | |
|---|---|
| Ultrasound | High frequency sound which is reflected from the tissues in a manner similar to radar |

### V

| | |
|---|---|
| Varicose veins | Tortuous dilated superficial veins |
| Vascular graft | Synthetic material used to bypass arteries. |
| Vein | A vessel taking blood from the organs and the limbs to the heart |

| | |
|---|---|
| Venography | An imaging process, involving the injection of X-ray opaque contrast material into a vein, in order to outline the venous system |
| V/Q scan | Ventilation perfusion scan – a test for pulmonary embolism |

**W**

| | |
|---|---|
| Warfarin | An orally active anticoagulant |

# INDEX

Acute arterial emboli ............................. 14–15
Acute thrombosis .................................... 66
Acutely ischaemic limb ......................... 65–66
Airline passengers .................................... 91
Amputation
    artificial limbs ................................. 58–59
    bypasses ............................................ 57
    complications .................................... 59
    consent ......................................... 58, 59
    diabetic feet .................................. 60–63
    feet .................................. 17, 57–58, 60
    gangrene ........................................... 58
    infection ............................................ 58
    ischaemic pain .................................. 58
    legs ......................................... 17, 19–20
    medical negligence .......................... 115
    prostheses ..................................... 58–59
    septicaemia ....................................... 58
    treatment of arterial
        disease ..................................... 57–59
Anatomy ................................................. 1–4
Aneurysms ............................ 9–12, 51–54, 75
Angiography .............................. 35–37, 74
Angioplasty ........................... 42–48, 55, 60
Anticoagulants ..................... 90–91, 93–94, 96–97, 105, 109–10
Aorta-iliac vessels ................... 33, 35, 55–57
Aortic aneurysm ................................. 51–54
Arterial disease ....................... 13–22, 25–39
Artificial limbs .................................... 58–59
Arteries ................................................ 6–7
    *See, also,* Investigation
    of venous disease;
    Treatment of arterial
    disease
    anterior tibial ................................ 72–93
    arterial disease .............................. 13–22
    arterial system ................................. 1–2
    arterial tree ......................................... 3
    arteriosclerosis ............................... 9–10
    arteriovenous
        malformations .................... 12, 70–71
    axillary ............................................ 113
    blocking .................................. 1–2, 9, 56
    blunt trauma .................................. 9, 18
    brachial ............................ 46–48, 60, 72
    broken bones ........................... 18–19, 113

    carotid ................................... 27, 49–51
    common iliac ................................ 20–21
    complications ................................. 114
    congenital disorders ........................ 12
    degenerative
        disorders ........................................ 9
    description ..................................... 1, 6
    dilation ............................................ 51
    disease ........................................ 13–23
    dislocation .................................... 113
    distended ........................................ 10
    emboli ............................................. 10
    expansive nature of ......................... 6
    external iliac ............................... 21–22
    femoral ................................... 18–19, 34, 56–57, 66, 113
    hardening ...................... 14, 16, 41, 116
    iliac ............................................. 20–23
    infective disorders ............................ 9
    laparoscopic injuries .................. 20–22
    leg ................................................... 13
    malformations ........................ 12, 70–71
    narrowing ......................... 9–10, 13, 27, 28, 41–42, 49, 117
    neoplastic disorders ....................... 12
    occlusion ............................ 28, 42, 46, 49, 55–56, 65, 113
    oxygen ........................................... 6–7
    pathology ..................................... 9–12
    physiology ..................................... 6–7
    popliteal .............................. 19–20, 37
    pulmonary ....................................... 7
    pulse ................................ 6, 18–20, 27, 59–60, 72–73, 113, 116
    reconstruction ..................... 19, 48, 109, 113–14
    renal .............................................. 113
    surgical damage ..................... 9, 113–14
    thrombosis ................................. 10, 66
    trauma ............................. 18–22, 113–14
    tumours .......................................... 12
Arteriography ...................... 14, 31–34, 42, 46, 62, 66, 72, 93
Arterio-portal shunt ............................. 32
Arteriosclerosis ...................... 9–10, 16, 41, 51–54, 65
Arterio-venous fistula ........................ 109
Arteriovenous
    malformations ......................... 12, 70–71

## Vascular Surgery

Assessments
    blood pressure ............................116
    causation ................................116–17
    delay ..........................................115
    deterioration..............................115
    experiments ..............................116
    investigations of
        arterial disease .....................26
    investigation of
        venous disease .....................78
    medico-legal ..........................115–17
    specialists .................................115
    surgery ......................................116
    treatment plans .........................116
    varicose veins ........................100–03
    veins .....................................115–17

Atheroma .........................................14

Atheromatous plaque ...................49–51

Atrial fibrillation ...............................72

Atrium ................................................1

Auscultation ................................27, 78

Axillary arteries ..............................113

Axillary hyperhidrosis ..................69–70

Balloon inflation
    technique ................................42, 45

Baro receptors ....................................6

Birth marks ..................................70–71

Blood,
    *see, also,* Blood pressure
    carbon dioxide .............................7
    clotting .........................5, 10, 14, 18,
                       65–66, 92,
                       94–95, 97

        description of ..............................5
        loss of ...........................................7
        oxygen .......................................71
        photoplethysmography .............79
        plasma .........................................5
        pooling ........................................6
        pulmonary embolism ................93
        red cells .......................................5
        sugar levels ...........................15–16
        transfusion ...............................114
        volume .........................................6
        white cells ....................................5

Blood pressure ................................1–2
    ankle brachial
        pressure index ...............28–29, 60
    arterial ......................................5–6
        disease .......................................13
    assessments ..............................116
    auscultation ................................27
    baro receptors ..............................6
    circulation ...................................6
    fall in .......................................5–6
    high .......................................1, 13
    loss of blood ................................6
    peripheral resistance ...................6
    pulmonary embolism ................97
    venous ..........................98, 112–13

Blunt trauma .................................9, 18

Brachial arteries .......................46–48, 72

Brachial pressure .......................28, 60

Broken bones ......................18–19, 113

Buerger's disease ..............................18

Bypasses
    acute thrombosis .......................66
    amputation ................................57
    angioplasty ................................55
    aorto-bifemoral .........................56
    aorto-iliac disease .................55–56
    arterial disease ......................55–57
    brachial injuries ........................48
    carotid arterial
        disease .....................................40
    complications ......................56, 57
    femoro-femoral .........................55
    femoro-popliteal ........................57
    grafts ..............................48, 55–55
    infection .....................................57
    legs ........................................55–57
    thrombosis ...............................112
    venous .....................................112
    warnings ...................................57

Capacitance vessels ............................6

Carbon dioxide ...................................7

Cardiac disease .................................13

Cardiac failure ....................................6

Carotid arteries .......................27, 49–51

Carotid body tumours .....................12

Carpal tunnel syndrome .............68–59

Catheterisation .......................42–48, 66

Cellulitis ..........................................14

126

# Index

Cerebrovascular
  disease..........................13, 13, 49–50
Cervical
  sympathectomy.................17–18, 67–70
Chambers ............................................1
Chemical sympathectomy.................67
Cholecystectomy..........................20–21
Circulation
  acutely ischaemic
    limbs.....................................65–66
  anatomy ........................................1
  bleeding....................................114
  blocking......................................10
  blood pressure ............................6
  capacitance vessels ....................6
  cardiac
    catheterisation.........................47
  clotting ......................5, 10, 14, 18,
                                            65–66, 92,
                                             94–95, 97
  compression ..............73, 91, 98, 113
  diabetes ......................................16
  diagram .......................................7
  dislocation.................................18
  emboli........................................14
  infections ..................................12
  legs............................................112
  lungs............................................1
  pathology................................9–12
  peripheral................................1, 6
  pulmonary ................................12
  temperature...............................27
  valve repairs........................111–12
  Volkmann's ischaemic
    contracture ..............................72
Claudication .....................13, 28, 41, 115
Clotting...............................5, 10, 14, 18,
                                            65–66, 92,
                                             94–95, 97
Common iliac arteries................20–21
Compartment
  syndrome............................72–73, 113
Compression ......................73, 91, 98, 99,
                                         105, 109, 113
Congenital disorders........................12
Congestive heart failure ....................6
Connective tissue
  disorders ................................16–17

Deep vein thrombosis.................87–92
  airline passengers ....................91
  anticoagulants...............89–91, 94,
                                              96–97
  bleeding................................90–91
  clotting .........................87–88, 94
  complications ......................88, 91
  compression ..............................91
  diagnosis ..............................82, 88
  duplex ultrasound
    imaging ............................82, 88
  extensive ....................................90
  leg injuries ....................13, 94–95
  multiple injuries
    leading to........................96–97
  occlusion ...................................90
  orthopaedics ..............................91
  post-thrombotic limbs ..............98
  prevention ...........................90–92
  prophylactic
    measures..........................91–92
  pulmonary embolism ..........93–97
  road traffic accidents ........94, 96–97
  subcutaneous heparin ........89–91
  superficial
    thrombophlebitis..........95, 102–03
  surgery .......................................91
  symptoms .......................22, 87–88
  treatment....................................89
  valves..........................................88
  varicose veins......................102–03
  venograms .....................84, 88, 89
  X-rays.........................................88
Degenerative disorders......................9
Diabetes.................................15–16, 28,
                                                 59–63
Diaphysial aclasis .............................72
Diathermy.........................................67
Digital subtraction
  angiography ....................35–37, 74
Digital subtraction
  techniques.................................93
Dislocation................................18, 113
Doppler ultrasound..............28–30, 59,
                                  78, 100, 113,
                                                 116
Duplex ultrasound
  imaging...............29–30, 60, 70–71,
                                  74, 82–84, 100,
                                  105, 110, 112,
                                                 116

ECGs ................................................28, 93
Elective embolisation ...........................32
Electrocardiograms .........................28, 93
Electrolytes...........................................28
Emboli ...............................13, 46, 92–97,
                                            102–03
    acute arterial................................14–15
    arteriosclerosis ..............................10
    arterio-venous
        malformations ......................71
    brachial artery ...............................72
    circulation ......................................14
    diagnosis..............................92–93, 97
    elective embolisation ...................32
    embolectomy.............................65–66
    embolisation............................32, 71
    illnesses, associated
        with.........................................15
    legs ..............................................14–15
    pulmonary...........................92–97, 102–03
    saddle .............................................65
    varicose veins..........................102–03
    Volkmann's ischaemic
        contracture ...........................72
Extosis ..................................................72

False aneurysms..............................10–12
Fasciotomy ...........................................73
Feet
    acutely ischaemic
        limbs.................................65–66
    amputation ....................17, 57–58, 60
    diabetes ....................................16, 59–63
    footwear .........................................61
    infection.........................................17
    nerve injuries...............................110
    Raynaud's disease .......................17
Femoral arteries .....................15, 18–19, 34,
                                        56–57, 66, 113
Femoral veins ..............................111, 112
Fibrinolytic system ..............................5
Fogarty catheter ..................................66

Gangrene .........................................18, 58
Glossary........................................119–24
Gynaecological surgery ..................21–22

Haemoglobin ........................................28
Haematoma ...........................72, 74, 93
Haemoptysis.........................................92
Hardening of the
    arteries..............................................14
Heparin ............................89–91, 93–94,
                                    96–97, 109–10
Hormones.............................................77
Horner's syndrome .........................67–68
Hyperhidrosis ..................................67–70
Hypertension,
    see Blood pressure

Iliac arteries ........................20–23, 55–57
Iliac embolectomy...............................15
Infective disorders
    antibiotics......................................74
    bypasses ........................................57
    debridement .................................60
    diabetes ...........................16, 59, 61–63
    feet..................................................17
    gangrene ..................................18, 58
    grafts ..............................................74
    microsclerotherapy ...................106
    Raynaud's disease .......................17
    septicaemia ....................................9
    surgery ..................................11–12, 74
    ulcers..............................................98
Investigation of arterial
    disease .......................................25–39
    ankle brachial
        pressure index ..................28–29, 60
    arteriography ..........................31–34
    auscultation .................................27
    diagnosis..................................25–26
    digital subtraction
        angiography......................35–37
    doppler ultrasound ..............28–30, 59
    duplex ultrasound
        imaging......................29–30, 60,
                                              70–71, 74
    examination.............................26–27
    history............................................26
    inspection......................................26
    legs .................................................25
    magnetic resonance
        imaging...........................38–39
    palpation .......................................27

# Index

routine tests .................................................28
ultrasound
    stethoscope...........................................28
Investigation of
  venous disease .........................................77–85
  auscultation ....................................................78
  Doppler ultrasound ............................78, 100
  duplex ultrasound
    imaging.....................................82–84, 100,
                                   112, 116
  examination........................................77–78
  history.............................................................77
  hormones ......................................................77
  inspection......................................................78
  palpation.......................................................78
  photoplethysmography .....................79–81
  strain gauge
    plethysmography...........................80–81
  ultrasound
    stethoscope...........................................78
  venography ............................................84–85
Ischaemic attacks ..........................................13, 49
Ischaemic contracture .................................71–73
Ischaemic pain.........................................58, 65–66
Joints......................................................................9

Keyhole surgery..........................................74–75

Laparoscopic injuries .................................20–23
Lasers .................................................................107
Legs
  acute arterial
    embolus ...........................................14–15
  acutely ischaemic
    limbs..................................................65–66
  amputation ......................................13, 19–20
  arterial disease .........................13–15, 25–26
  bypasses ..................................................55–57
  cellulitis .........................................................14
  circulation ...................................................112
  claudication .................................13, 28, 41
  deep vein thrombosis ....................13, 94–95
  embolism .................................................13–14
  injuries....................................................94–95
  inspection......................................................78
  palpation.......................................................27
  photoplethysmography............................79
  post-thrombotic limbs ................................98
  rest pain.........................................................13
  strain gauge
    plethysmography...........................80–81

surgery ..........................................................52
temperature .................................................27
valves ..........................................................112
Lipodermatosclerosis.........................................98
Lumbar sympathectomy .............................14, 70

Magnetic resonance
    imaging.............................................38–39, 74
Medico-legal assessments ........................115–17
Microangiopathy ................................................16
Microsclerotherapy ...................................105–06

Neoplastic disorders .........................................12
Nerve injuries..................................49–50, 59–60,
                                68–69, 101–03,
                                        110, 111

Neuropathy .................................................59–60

Occlusion .........................................28, 42, 46, 49,
                                    55–56, 65, 78,
                                    90, 112, 113
Ophthalmoscopes..............................................27
Orthopaedics .............................................91, 96–97
Osteomyelitis...............................................14–15
Oxygen .....................................................6–7, 71

Palma operations .............................................112
Palpation ..................................................27, 78
Paraesthesia ..................................................68–69
Pathology ....................................................9–12
Percutaneous transluminal
    angioplasty ............................................43, 75
Peripheral circulation......................................1, 6
Peripheral vascular
    disease ...............................................13, 65–66
Photoderm........................................................107
Photoplethysmography ....................................79
Physiology ..................................................5–7
Plasma ................................................................5
Plethysmography ........................................80–81
Popliteal arteries .................................19–20, 37
Popliteal veins ..................................................110
Posterior tibial veins..........................................82
Post-thrombotic limbs.......................................98

Presentation of
    vascular disease ......................13–23
Prophylactic measures ................91–92
Prostheses .......................................59–60
Pulmonary embolism ....................92–97
Pulmonary system
    arteries ..................................................7
    circulation ...........................................1
    embolism ..............................92–97, 102–03
Pulse ................................................6, 19–20, 27,
                                59–60, 72–73,
                                113, 116

Raynaud's disease ...........................16–18, 69, 71
Reconstruction ................................19, 23, 48, 58,
                                60–62, 109–14
Red cells .................................................5
Reflux ...............................................78–79, 94
Renal arteries .................................113
Repair of valves ...........................111–12
Replacement of valves ................111–12
Rest pain .........................................13
Retroperitoneal
    haematomas .................................93
Road accidents ...............................73, 94, 96–97

Saddle emboli .................................65
Sapheno-femoral
    junctions .......................................83
Sapheno-femoral
    ligation ..........................................95
Saphenous nerve
    injuries ..........................................103, 111
Saphenous veins .............................103, 110, 111,
                                112
Sclerotherapy ..................................99–100,
                                102–06, 111
Seldinger technique .......................31
Sensory nerve damage ..................59–60, 103
Septicaemia ....................................9, 58
Skin ulceration ...............................106–07
Smoking
    arterial disease ............................26
    Buerger's disease ........................18
    X-rays ............................................28

Spasm ..............................................16–18
Stents ...............................................42–43, 74
Stethoscopes
    arterial disease ............................27
    ultrasound ...................................28–30, 59, 78
Strain gauge
    plethysmography .......................80–81
Strokes ............................................10, 13, 49–50
Subtalar joint
    arthrodesis ..................................96
Superficial
    thrombophlebitis ........................95, 102–03,
                                105
Surgery, *see, also,* Bypasses
    acutely ischaemic
        limbs .......................................65–66
    aortic aneurysm .........................51–52
    arteries ..........................................9, 113–14
    assessment ...................................116
    bleeding .......................................74
    bypass ..........................................55–57, 112–13
    cervical
        sympathectomy ....................69
    claudication ................................41
    common iliac arteries .................20–22
    complications .............................73–75, 116
    debridement ...............................60
    deep vein thrombosis ................91
    embolectomy ..............................65–66
    fitness for .....................................74
    grafts ............................................74
    gynaecological ............................21–22
    haematoma .................................74
    infections .....................................11–12, 74
    keyhole ........................................74–75
    laparoscopic injuries .................20–22
    legs ................................................52
    nerve injuries ..............................49–50
    Palma ............................................112
    politeal fossa ...............................110
    strokes .........................................49–50
    sympathectomy .........................67–70
    treatment of arterial
        disease ....................................73–74
    valves ...........................................112
    varicose veins .............................99, 100–04,
                                110, 111
    veins .............................................9, 109,
                                112–13
    warnings .....................................49–50, 52,
                                57, 73–74,
                                101

# Index

Sympathetic overactivity............................69–70
Sympathectomy ......................14, 17–18, 66–70
Symptomatic chronic
    colecystitis.....................................................20

Temperature ........................................................27
Thorascopes ........................................................67
Thrombo obliterative
    disease .............................................................18
Thrombophlebitis ...............................95, 102–05
Thrombosis ...................................10, 22, 42, 66, 87–88, 109, 112

    *See, also*, Deep vein thrombosis

Tourniquets ...................................................72–73
Transient ischaemic
    attacks.......................................................13, 49
Trauma to arteries ..........................18–22, 113–14
Trauma to veins ......................................23, 109–13
Traumatic disorders .................................9, 18–23
Treatment of arterial
    disease ......................................................41–75
    acutely ischaemic
        limbs........................................................65–66
    amputation ...............................................57–59
    angioplasty ..............................................42–48
    aortic aneurysm ......................................51–54
    arterio-venous
        malformations ...............................70–71
    bypass surgery........................................55–57
    diabetic feet .............................................59–63
    endarterectomy.......................................49–50
    intermittent
        claudication............................................41
    surgical
        complications......................................73–74
    sympathectomy ......................................66–70
    Volkmann's ischaemic
        contracture .........................................71–73
Treatment of venous
    disease ......................................................87–98
    deep vein thrombosis ............................87–92
    post-thrombotic
        limbs.........................................................98
    pulmonary embolism ............................92–97
True aneurysms ..................................................10

Tumours ..............................................................12
Turbulence ..........................................................27

Ulceration
    diabetic foot......................................16, 59, 61
    duplex ultrasound
        imaging ....................................................82
    endarterectomy................................................49
    infection...........................................................98
    microsclerotherapy ................................106–07
    post-thrombotic
        limbs.........................................................98
    skin............................................................106–07
    sympathectomy .......................................66–67
    valve repairs..................................................112
    varicose veins ................................22, 99, 104, 106–07
Ultrasound
    aortic aneurysm ............................................51
    doppler.........................................28–30, 59, 78, 100, 113
    duplex .........................................29–30, 60, 70–71, 82–84, 74, 100, 105, 110, 112, 116
    imaging .........................................29–30, 82–84
    stethoscopes ...........................................28, 78
Urea ......................................................................28

Valves ......................................1–2, 6, 84, 98, 111–12
Varicose veins .........................................77, 99–107
    anticoagulants....................................105, 111
    appearance.....................................................99
    assessment ..............................................100–03
    bleeding.........................................................101
    bruising...................................................101–02
    compression .......................................99, 104–05
    deep vein
        thrombosis ......................................102–03
    deep veins, injury to ..........................110–11
    Doppler ultrasound
        stethoscopes ..........................................100
    duplex ultrasound
        imaging............................100, 105, 110
    femoral veins................................................111
    grafts..............................................................111
    infection........................................................106
    junctions.......................................................101
    lasers .............................................................107
    microsclerotherapy .............................105–06

## Vascular Surgery

nerve injuries....................101–03
photoderm...........................107
photoplethysmography...........79
pulmonary embolism..........102–03, 105
reconstruction.................110, 111
saphenous nerve
    injuries........................103, 111
sclerotherapy......................99–100, 102–07, 111
sensory nerve
    damage..........................103
skin ulceration..................106–07
superficial
    thrombophlebitis...........102–03, 105
surgery..............................99, 100–04, 110, 111
symptoms.............................99
thrombophlebitis................102–05
treatment...........................99–100, 100–07, 110
ulceration..........................22, 99, 104, 106–07
venous disease......................22
Vaso-spastic conditions...........67
    See, also, Raynaud's disease
Veins.................................6–7
    See, also, Deep vein thrombosis;
    Investigation of venous disease;
    Treatment of venous disease; Varicose veins
    arteries..........................1
    arteriovenous
        malformations............12, 70–71
    blood pressure..............98, 112–13
    bypass surgery..................112–13
    carbon dioxide.....................7
    clotting..........................10
    congenital disorders............12
    deep..............................2
    degenerative
        disorders....................10
    description.......................6
    dilation.........................10
    disease...........................13, 22–23, 77–85
    duplication.......................2
    femoral..........................83, 85, 111, 112
    hums.............................78

malformations....................12, 70–71
medico-legal
    assessment..................115–17
narrowing...........................78
obstruction......................80, 113
occlusion........................78, 90, 112
oxygen...............................7
pathology..........................9–12
peripheral.........................2, 13
physiology.........................6–7
popliteal..........................110
posterior tibial...................83
reconstruction.................23, 109–13
reflux............................78–79, 94
sapheno-femoral
    junction........................83
saphenous........................103, 110, 112
superficial.........................2
surgery..........................9, 109, 112–13
thrombosis.........................22
trauma..........................23, 109–113
valves............................1–2, 6, 98, 111–12
venous disease...................22–23
venous system.......................2
venous tree.........................4
volume of blood in..................6
Vena cava............................2
Venography......................84–85, 89
Venous disease...................22–23
Ventricles..........................1
Vessels.............................6–7
    See, also, Arteries; Veins
Vibration white finger.............16
Volkmann's ischaemic
    contracture....................71–73

White cells..........................5

X-rays
    arteriography................31–34, 93
    cervical
        sympathectomy...............68
    deep vein thrombosis.............95
    digital subtraction
        angiography.................35–37
    pulmonary embolism............92–93
    smoking..........................28
    venography.......................84